ELON MUSK
The Kid Who Touched the Stars

Copyright © 2021. All rights reserved by Wild Soccer USA Inc.

No part of this book may be reproduced or transmitted in any form or by any means, electronic or mechanical, including photocopying, recording, or by any information storage or retrieval system, without written permission from Sole Books. For information regarding permission, write to Sole Books, P.O. Box 10445, Beverly Hills, CA 90213.

Editor: Y Ginsberg

Proof-editor: Marc Murphy-Robinson

Cover design: Mirko Pohle

Layout: Lazar Kackarovski

Library of Congress Cataloging-in-Publication data available.

Print ISBN: 978-1-938591-84-6
ebook ISBN: 978-1-938591-85-3

Published by Sole Books, an imprint of Wild Soccer USA, Beverly Hills, California.

Printed in the United States of America.

First edition September 2021.

www.solebooks.com

Elon Musk

The Kid Who Touched the Stars

by
Kevin Ashby

Sole
BOOKS

"People should pursue what they're passionate about. That will make them happier than pretty much anything else."

~ Elon Musk ~

Perfect Landing

A huge rocket hissed on the launchpad. Still as stone, like a monster getting ready to pounce. Clouds boiled out of it like breath.

Overhead was a dark sky, frothy with stars. It was December 22nd, 2015, and the time was 7:29 pm local time.

"T-minus 60," a voice said, loud and crisp. "All systems go."

Cape Canaveral's mission control was calm yet busy, crowded with men and women monitoring their computer screens. In exactly one minute, the SpaceX Falcon rocket was scheduled to take off.

Elon Musk stood there, watching. His heart thumped. His Falcon rockets had flown successfully into space for seven years. But today, he was about to reach another milestone. It was the first time in space exploration's history that the first stage of an orbital rocket was supposed to land back where it started from.

The landing pad was marked by two circles, one inside the other, surrounded by laser lights. The lights beamed columns of brightness straight up into the sky.

There was tension in the air. The landing system had worked in tests – but never before in a live mission. His excitement grew as time passed.

"T-minus ten," the voice announced calmly, continuing the count.

The mission control's floor shuddered as the mighty rumble of the rocket began. Falcon soared into the night, firing off its nine Merlin engines.

"Night launches are the best!" a woman next to Elon muttered. He nodded back, his gaze fixed on the screens.

Falcon was invisible when its burn ended. Everyone gazed at the screens. The second stage, called Kestrel, ignited and sped beyond it into space. Meanwhile, Falcon began plunging back to Earth. Measurements were sent at light speed between its thrusters and launch control. Elon scanned the data.

Separation – check.

Free-fall – on track.

Landing thrusters – alight.

Suddenly, they could hear the roar.

"It's coming," Elon half-shouted, half-breathed.

He couldn't stay still any longer. He grabbed his jacket and ran, bursting from mission control into the cool of the night. Dozens of people raced with him. No one could help it. They were all too excited.

They could see Falcon 9, a small blaze of thrusters, coming down through the air. It loomed closer and closer. It was pointing straight up, dead center above the landing stage. They could see the landing legs unfolding. Four giant pillars came out from the engines.

The Kid Who Touched the Stars

"Too fast!" Elon warned suddenly, grabbing the shoulders of the nearest engineer. "Don't you think?"

It *looked* too fast, as if the giant cylinder would smash into the ground. For a second, Elon imagined the rocket swallowed in a storm of vicious flame. Then it slowed, tiny boosts from the thrusters kicking in.

Slowed.

Slowed.

Hovered.

Touched the ground, as gently as a hand laid on a head.

The thrusters killed. There was silence.

Falcon stood there – stable, upright, whole.

For a moment, Elon couldn't believe it. Then a roar erupted from his chest. He leaped and punched in the air. Someone grabbed him, and they started dancing. He could hear the bellow of cheering engineers coming from mission control.

He stared at the recovered machine and smiled.

He took hold of a microphone.

"It's amazing, isn't it? What a sight. It's the next level. I'm lost for words!"

Everyone cheered. "It just shows. Working hard, using intelligence and imagination, we can achieve the impossible. And you *know* we're going to do it again!"

He looked around. Everyone's faces were filled with joy – and determination.

"We're going to get to Mars."

More cheers. Elon lifted his arms above his head. Some of them chanted his name. He let his hands drop.

"OK. We definitely should party. We'll meet again tomorrow."

He handed the microphone off and stepped back. He couldn't stop smiling.

Out of the corner of his eye, he saw an electric car roll up, as quiet as a mother humming. It was a Tesla X. The doors swung up over the car's back, like wings. His five sons tumbled out and ran toward him, followed by Tallulah, his wife. He caught Saxon, one of the younger boys, in his arms. Tallulah came and kissed him.

As he stood surrounded by the people he loved, he thought about his amazing journey. And then he looked up at the sky.

"Mars, here I come," he whispered.

CHAPTER ONE

Far Away

"Elon! Coo – eee!"

"C'mon Elon!"

Maye Musk looked at her three children and smiled.

"Let him be," she said softly.

Kimbal and Tosca, Elon's little brother and sister, sighed.

"We want to play, Mom!" Tosca pouted. She was four.

"Yeah, Mom," Kimbal agreed. "You told us we were supposed to include Elon. We're going to play catch. Is he going to join in?"

Kimbal, who was five, bounced a tennis ball eagerly. Suddenly, he threw it hard, and it pinged toward Tosca. She shrieked and threw her arms up. It stuck in her fingers. She stared, then her face lit up in triumph.

"I caught it, Mom. Look!"

"That's great, darling!" their mother said.

Six-year-old Elon half heard but didn't say anything. He thought it was nice his little sister caught the ball. She almost never did. But he was concentrating. Thinking about something else.

They were in Maye's backyard in Durban, South Africa. It was mid-spring of 1977, and a light breeze ran off the sea. Elon was thinking about the breeze. He was concentrating so hard that everything else seemed to disappear. He realized that the breeze didn't make straight lines, but swirls, like water going down the plug. Lots of swirls pushing against each other. He could see them in his imagination. It was amazing.

"Let's just the two of us play," Kimbal said to Tosca, and they ran off, joking.

Mom stayed to watch Elon. She loved the faraway look he got when he was concentrating. He could get so excited at the things he imagined. She wondered what was in his head right then.

Suddenly Elon blinked, as if his concentration was over.

"Hi, Mom!" he said, a broad smile on his face. He got up from the lawn and joined her. She looked at him fondly.

"Kimb and Tosc are playing catch," she said. "Want to join them?"

Elon cocked his head to one side, as if this needed lots of thinking. Then he shook it.

"Do you want to play with *me*?" Maye asked.

He shook his head again. "I want to hear about Granddad."

He meant Grandpa Haldeman, Mom's father. He was tall, like Mom, and told fantastic stories. He'd died three years ago, and Elon missed him and his stories.

"Tell me about the lion again," Elon said.

The Kid Who Touched the Stars

Maye agreed. They sat opposite each other, and Elon looked at her in anticipation. She smiled. He loved her voice.

"There is a legend that there is a lost, ruined city in the Kalahari desert. My mom and dad – Granny and Grandpa – believed this legend was true, so they used to drive off with me and Uncle Scott and Aunt Kaye every summer looking for it. We went in a truck and took everything with us: pots, pans, fire, food, clothes, books, and *one toy* each. We drove out into the desert where there are no roads and only the sun and stars to tell us where we were. But we had our compass and maps, so we never got lost."

"Live dangerously, carefully!" Elon nodded.

"That's right." Maye nodded back. "Well, once, we had a guide with us, a guy named Hendrik. Hendrik liked to sleep next to the campfire. He told us animals would never go near a fire." Elon was smiling at that point because he remembered how Grandpa always paused and laughed quietly when he got to that bit of the story. Maye raised her eyebrows knowingly at Elon. Elon eye-rolled, as if to say *silly Hendrik*.

"Early one morning, we heard a noise. There was a lion. Right there in the camp. And the lion just swaggered right on over to the fire where Hendrik was. 'Hendrik,' Grandpa hissed. 'Wake up. A lion!' You should have seen Hendrik. He leaped up, throwing off his blanket like someone had put ants in his bottom. And then he just *waved* at the lion and said, 'Go away!' Softly, like this." She whispered, "Go Away!"

"You can't scare off a lion by just saying *Go Away*!" Elon eye-rolled again.

"No." Maye nodded. "But luckily, by then, Grandpa had his gun and fired a couple of shots over the lion's head. Then he got in the truck and chased the lion. The lion didn't go far, mind. He just sat and watched us from a sand dune the whole morning. In the end, *we* were the ones who went away."

"Grandpa knew, didn't he, that the lion can't have been hungry?" Elon commented. "He was just curious, and he wanted to show these new animals that were in his country – us – who was in charge."

Maye nodded.

"I think if it was Dad, he would have tried to shoot the lion," Elon said. "And that would have made the lion mad. That would be living dangerously, *dangerously*."

"Maybe," Maye said.

"Grandpa's way is better," Elon observed quickly. Then he beamed at his mom. "*I'm* going to find lost cities when I grow up. Or maybe I'll fly up to the moon and build cities up there. I'll make sure to take everything I need."

Maye smiled again. Elon's dad and mom were separated. Elon knew that saying his name made his mom sad, and that was why he changed the subject.

"I think I'll go and play catch now," he said. "You know, I was thinking about the wind just then. I want to see if the ball reacts like I think it will."

"OK, honey," Maye said. Then she whispered. "Just don't tell them you're doing an experiment! Pretend you're just playing."

Elon beamed again. "OK. But if I'm right, I'll have to let them know. If I find out a lot, I can live dangerously, carefully, like Grandpa. And also I can help Tosca catch better because I can help her know what the wind will do to the ball."

He ran off.

Maye watched them all play. Elon cocked his head like he was listening to the breeze before throwing and catching. It seemed to work. He was doing better than the other times they'd played catch.

After a while, he ran back. "I was right, Mom. The wind goes in circles. It's tricky."

Then he ran back to the game.

CHAPTER TWO

Genius Boy

"We were doing playdough and painting footprints, and I got every color of paint all over my feet and then Miss made me wash it off, but I bet there's some still there. I can step on you too and make you all painty!"

Elon and Kimbal looked at each other while Tosca babbled on. They were all together, coming out of their elementary school gates. Tosca had only just started, and she was excited.

"Race you!" Elon shouted and hared off. Kimbal charged after him straight away.

"Wait for me!" Tosca wailed. "I was *telling* you!"

When he got to a corner, Elon waited for everyone to catch up. He felt responsible. Impatient, too.

He looked up at the sky. It was a beautiful spring day again. A few wisps of cloud drifted by. *Stratus*, he said to himself. A picture from the *Encyclopedia Britannica* sprang into his mind. He'd read the page a few weeks before. The page had diagrams of all the kinds of clouds and their names. Stratus were the little flat clouds, though sometimes they could cover the whole sky.

"ELON!" Kimbal bellowed. "Are we crossing this road now?"

Elon shook out of his thoughts and nodded. "Do you know that clouds are water?" he announced. "Water that's in the air? Tiny, tiny droplets that join around very tiny dust and moss seeds and animals that the wind catches and blows around really high?"

He *saw* it in his head – the individual specks of water too small to see with your eyes. Rising from the ground, finding the bits of stuff. They got bigger and bigger till there was a cloud. It was happening all around them right then. It was amazing. He wanted the others to share.

"Whatever, Genius Boy!" Tosca rolled her eyes. "Look at my *feet*."

She stuck a leg in the air and hopped and pulled off her trainer. The underneath of her foot *did* have lots of little specks of paint.

Elon grinned. "No cars," he said. "You better walk properly across the road right now."

He strode off before she could put her trainer back on. She scowled when she reached the other side.

"Now I've got all dusty!"

"Here." Elon lifted Tosca's foot up, dusted it, and fixed the trainer in place. The puffs of dust hung in the air. He swished them with his hands. "Look. It's going up to make clouds."

Tosca watched for a while. Then she giggled and sprinted off along the pavement, laughing back at him.

"I'm going to beat you home, Genius Boy!"

He shook his head. Genius Boy was Tosca's nickname for him. She said he deserved it because he always knew *everything* about *everything*. She said it like that was a little bit wrong. But why would anyone *not* want to know things? That was why he loved reading the *Encyclopedia Britannica*. You found things out.

He raced off. Kimbal was already level with Tosca. When he caught her up, he goosed her as he went by. She yelled.

As soon as they got home, he pulled one of the big, fat, red books of the *Encyclopedia Britannica* off the shelf and flopped onto the living room sofa. He flipped through the pages and stopped on one without looking to see the page number. He started reading. After a few words, he stopped. He recognized these words. He shut his eyes, remembering, then opened them and looked down the page to check. Yep, he remembered it alright. He must have already read that page. He could do that, remember something exactly as soon as he'd read and understood it once. He skipped a few pages and started again. He knew that one already, too.

"Elon, come and have your tea!" Maye called.

He sat down and started chewing the peanut butter and lettuce sandwiches his Mom had made. He sipped at the glass of OJ next to his plate.

"Mom," he said, "did you know clouds are made of water?"

Kimbal and Tosca glanced at each other.

"Yes, I did, honey," Maye replied. "Evaporated water droplets from the sea and rivers and plants, condensed around all the invisible matter in the air. Did you learn that at school today?"

"I read it," Elon said, shaking his head.

The Kid Who Touched the Stars

"In the *Encyclopedia Britannica*?" Maye asked, nodding. "You have a great memory, Elon."

He nodded, smiling. He knew she was right, and it made him proud.

Later on, in bed, he lay awake thinking. It was really dark. The stratus clouds had covered the whole sky outside, so there were no stars or moon. They didn't have lights in the garden or on the street, either. It made it so dark you couldn't even see your own hand if you held it in front of your eyes.

"Elon? Elon? Are you awake?" It was Tosca, her voice quavering, outside his door.

He got up and went to open it.

"It's too dark," she whimpered. "There's a monster."

"Come in here," Elon whispered back. "I'll sit with you."

She took his hand.

"You know what," he said as they sat on the bed. "I used to be scared of the dark, too. I thought it was monsters, just like you. But then I realized something."

"What, Genius Boy?" Tosca murmured, snuggling against him.

"Well, it's simple. The dark isn't a *something*. It's just the *absence* of light." He squeezed his arm around her shoulder. "Do you get that? It's something *not* being there, not a thing itself."

Tosca sniffled. "Why is that not scary? Not-things are *bad*."

"No, Tosca." Elon chuckled softly. "How can they be? Not-things don't exist. They're not there, so there's nothing to be scared about. Dark is just *not* light. It's not there."

"I'm still scared," Tosca muttered. But she was breathing softer.

Her eyes shut, then her head fell on the pillow and she fell asleep.

Elon smiled. It was true about the dark, and it meant you needn't be scared. He wished he could get Tosca to see that.

He laid her head carefully on the pillow and wrapped the covers around them both. Then he settled down himself. He drifted off to sleep almost at once.

CHAPTER THREE

The Bookstore

Elon sat looking out of his primary school window, bored and impatient. He wanted to be somewhere else.

"Elon Musk!" Miss threw her voice across the room. "I thought I told you to read ahead!"

Elon held up his textbook, open at the last page. "I finished," he said flatly.

His exercise book was already with her. She *wasn't* marking it.

"Revise, then," she replied sternly. "Go back to the beginning!"

"*Miss* ..." Elon begged, then stopped.

He decided not to tell her he had a photographic memory and only needed to read the textbook once to remember everything in it.

He flipped the pages back and made a big show of smoothing page one down. His eyes skimmed the words. It was elementary science. There were *so many* questions the book didn't answer. It made him fidgety.

The bell went a minute later. Elon threw the textbook into his bag and stood by his desk before anyone else moved. He jigged to and fro in his eagerness to be off. Everyone else got up. Elon could swear the teacher looked at him and waited a whole minute before dismissing the class. He literally stampeded out of the door.

It was a bright, crisp afternoon. He was free to make his own way home.

For Elon, that meant only one thing.

He raced along the street away from the school gates, bag swinging over his shoulder. When he got to the crossroads, he just about remembered to look before launching across without a pause. He skidded to a stop five minutes later outside a shop with a double door and large windows stacked with books. Every one of them looked as delicious as ice cream.

He plunged inside, licking his lips, and headed past the counter, upstairs, to his favorite section. As soon as he got there, his eyes danced across the books' spines. He flung his bag down and ran his finger along the shelf, deciding which to read.

The Hitchhiker's Guide to the Galaxy. He loved that one. He tipped it into his hand, then carried on. A minute later, he was clutching a whole stack of books. Five comics, two fiction books, and an advanced physics textbook.

He sank down against the wall next to the shelves and started reading. On his right, next to his school bag, was his pile of unread books. On his left, a quarter of an hour later, another pile started – the books that he had finished reading from the first pile.

Outside, the sun advanced slowly through the sky. Cars began to gather as the afternoon wore on. The shop assistant wandered upstairs, stared at Elon, smiled, and walked down again. Everyone in the shop knew Elon. He came two or three times a week. The faraway look he had once he was lost in a book made them all smile.

Elon was oblivious to all of that. The pages of his books turned like the ticking of a clock. His eyes drank in each page as deeply and easily as breaths of cool, fresh air. The comics went through his hands first, each one devoured and transferred onto the left-hand pile. Then the *Hitchhiker's Guide to the Galaxy* series. Then the physics book.

He was halfway through the last book when the shop assistant climbed the stairs again.

"Elon!" he called out, softly but firmly.

Elon's face turned slowly upwards, blinking.

"It's time to go," the assistant told him, pointing through the window. "We're closing."

The lights had come on in the streets outside. The hum of rush-hour traffic echoed faintly through the glass.

Elon smiled, guiltily. "I lost track …"

"I know, young man," the assistant said with a laugh. "I don't think I ever saw someone spoon books down the way you do. Off you go home now. No doubt I'll see you again soon enough."

Elon picked up his pile of books and slotted each one back into place on the shelves. The shop assistant stood by the door, keys in hand, as Elon left the shop, nodding in thanks.

Elon breathed in the evening air. His eyes were glittering.

CHAPTER FOUR

The Gift

"I want a personal computer," Elon told Kimbal. They were in Elon's bedroom. "Do you know what that is?"

Kimbal was reading a comic. He wasn't listening.

"It's like a TV," Elon went on, louder. "But it has this thing called a keyboard and you can make anything you imagine come up on the screen. You write instructions with the keyboard, and the screen makes pictures like you imagined. *Anything*, Kimb. Do you understand?"

Kimbal said he did, but he wasn't listening.

"Doesn't that sound cool?" Elon insisted. "Uncle Scott talked about it."

Kimbal turned away. Elon felt disappointed by his brother's response. He'd seen a computer a few days before, for the first time. It was in the electrical goods shop, next to all the speakers and graphic equalizers and radios and record-players and cassette decks. He asked the salesperson what it was. "You can type documents on it, make programs that run calculations, play games, that sort of thing," the man explained. He said that it would change the world.

It sounded awesome. Elon was mesmerized. A personal computer. PC. He couldn't leave the store and kept hovering around it. He wanted to know everything about it and to own it.

He decided to ask his dad for one. His dad, Errol, was an engineer. He lived in a really big house in another city, Pretoria. After his parents' divorce, Maye Musk and the kids had moved to Durban, but once a month, they flew back to visit Dad.

Elon thought he could tell him that computers were tools, like you had in engineering. He would say, *I'm ten. I should be learning to make real things by now, not just building Meccano.*

A month later, Maye came to the airport to pick the kids up. Elon and his brother and sister had spent the weekend with their Dad. Elon almost forgot about the computer, but before they left, his dad had handed him the bag with the box.

"Here's that Commodore VIC-20 you wanted, Elon," he said. "It's not real engineering. It doesn't build anything in the real world." And then he said, "I hope you won't waste time playing silly games."

Typical Dad, Elon thought. *Make you feel what you wanted was wrong.* But he'd bought him the computer, anyway. It was probably Grandma Musk, his dad's mom, who swung it. She played Scrabble with Elon a lot, and he'd told her all about the computer and what it could do.

"It sounds like something to make you think logically and anticipate a long way ahead," she said.

Exactly, Grandma, Elon thought.

Elon was so excited; he couldn't wait to get home.

The computer came with a booklet that taught him how to program it.

As soon as they pulled up on Mom's drive, Elon got out of the car and headed for the stairs.

"We're eating first," Mom said, knowing he wanted to run into his room and open the box. Elon looked at her. He knew he had to give up and wait a bit.

Peanut butter sandwiches. OJ. As ever. With Dad, it was usually a barbecue that his cook prepared. Elon gobbled them down impatiently.

"Genius Boy lectured Grandma," Tosca piped up.

Elon shot her a look. "Grandma got her facts wrong! I couldn't help it." He wished people getting things wrong didn't irritate him so much. He'd lost school friends over that. Grandma was brainy, like Dad. She didn't often make mistakes.

"You should see Grandma's face when Elon recites the *Encyclopedia Britannica*," Kimbal said with a giggle.

They were proud of his memory – though everyone told him that no one likes a know-all.

Mom ruffled Elon's hair. "Tell me about this computer."

"I'm going to teach myself programming," Elon enthused. "It'll be great. I'll create games. Also maybe something for your diet customers. Just tell me what'll be useful. I can do it!"

His mom was a dietician.

She smiled. "OK," she said. "I'll think about that."

Elon looked like he was itching to go.

"Go on." Mom laughed. "Go and play with your computer."

Three days later, in the morning, Tosca was hammering on Elon's bedroom door.

"Genius Boy?" she yelled.

It was a bright day. Birdsong and the hiss of a few cars punctuated the swell of the sea.

"Genius Boy!" Tosca yelled again. "Mom says get *downstairs* for breakfast."

Tosca liked nothing better than being the one giving orders. It happened rarely. When Elon made no noise, she decided he'd overslept, and it was time for a joke. Noiselessly, she inched the door open and tiptoed across the room to bellow in his ear.

But Elon was up, at his desk, staring at the monitor of his computer. Line after line of green letters and numbers streamed up the screen. He was in the same shorts and t-shirt as when they'd come home three days ago. One leg was on his desk, and the programming book was on his lap, open at the last page.

Tosca stamped her foot. "Elon!"

He stank. She made a face. His hair was mussed and sweaty like someone had spattered cooking oil everywhere.

"What do you want?" He turned around, smiling. That was annoying because Tosca wanted to give him hell – but his freckles and big round eyes just made her want to give him a hug. He *never* got mad at her teasing.

"Mom says breakfast is ready," she repeated.

"Could you, um, maybe bring some up?" Elon tried. "It's just – I'm almost done with the programming, and I want to show you. I've made something for each of you. Look."

He pushed his chair away so she could see the screen. A single green square blinked inside an oblong box.

"Type your name in the box and hit the return key." Elon pointed. "That one."

As soon as she did, the letters of her name began moving and multiplying across the screen. They turned into a star, then a tree, then bursting fireworks. Eventually, they settled into the outline of a dress, a horse, an ice cream, and the beach. Underneath were the words: *A Picture of You. My Little Sister. Love Elon.*

Tosca's eyes shone.

"Like it?" Elon beamed. "Get me breakfast?"

"Yes!"

She ran out to tell everyone what he was up to.

As he watched her go, he felt happy, though he hadn't slept for three days. He had gone through the whole programming book in one session, and now he knew everything about writing programs in the BASIC language. It was like Grandma had said. All logic. The animation for Tosca was two days old. He'd written a game for Kimbal and a cool calculator for Mom. He couldn't wait to do more complicated things.

Tosca came back in with his breakfast. He ruffled her hair. She stuck out her tongue.

"Mom says you'll have to wash your things up *yourself.*"

But when he finished eating, all he could think of was sleep.

CHAPTER FIVE

Foundation

Elon huddled in his favorite corner of the bookshop. He was reading *Foundation's Edge*, the fourth book in Isaac Asimov's *Foundation* series. A handful of *National Geographic* magazines lay open around him as well. Elon could see them all at once.

He'd read the magazines before, but the book was new. He had waited for it impatiently, ever since he heard that Mr. Asimov was working on new Foundation stories. The first three, *Foundation*, *Foundation and Empire,* and *Second Foundation,* were some of his favorite books. He was so excited that Mr. Asimov was writing more. Now, at last, the book was here. It was late afternoon on a dull July day. The sky was already darkening to midwinter twilight.

He devoured the book, looking up to gaze at the magazines every few minutes.

To look at him, Elon was just an eleven-year-old kid scrunched up in a room that looked down on cars and shoppers. But really, he was not in the bookshop at all. He was not even on planet Earth.

Foundation's Edge took his mind far, far away, thousands of years into the future. The characters were in spaceships that flew faster than light between stars millions and millions of miles from each other. Elon flew with them. They were searching for each other, and for a secret that would save thousands of planets from wars and suffering. Elon searched with them. He was enthralled.

The magazines drew Elon's mind away from the bookstore too. They were about real space missions, to planets in Earth's solar system and to the space station hundreds of miles up in the sky.

One picture was of the planet Mars. Red dusty ground disappeared into a flat white sky that went as far as the camera could see. Rocks littered the dust like smashed plates. The picture was taken by the Viking lander, in 1976, when Elon was only five years old. When he looked at it, his heart beat faster. It was magnificent.

Another picture showed Jupiter. Jupiter was the next planet out from Mars. It was the biggest planet. You could fit over 1,300 Earths into its vast globe of gas. In the picture, Jupiter's surface swirled in bands of mixed blue, orange, and white, like a piece of marble. Moons floated like drops of blood against its background. That picture was taken by Voyager Two, in 1979.

The picture of Saturn was the newest. Saturn was the next planet after Jupiter. It was also unimaginably huge. Its sphere was pale blue and orange, like Durban's midwinter sunset. Sharp black and orange rings went around it.

Elon thought about the Voyager spaceships really and truly hurtling through the empty blackness of space. They had traveled for more than half his own life. While he went to school and played, they went on and on through space. They were still going on. In three and a half years, Voyager would reach Uranus, the seventh planet out from the sun. Three and a half years after that, it would get to the eighth planet, Neptune. He would just be coming to the end of school.

He turned back to the story. The characters had found a new planet around a new sun. The planet was green, and it was called Gaia. All the trees and animals and people on it could talk to each other. The characters had to decide whether every planet should join that one.

He looked up again. This time, he gazed at the article about the American space shuttle. It looked like the kind of airplane you could make out of a piece of paper – but massive. It was strapped on the back of two huge rockets. The rockets were surrounded by steam, ready for takeoff.

He closed his eyes. The first space shuttle landing had been shown on TV. The majestic glider came down through a haze of heat. It seemed to take forever. Its nose angled up into the sky just a little. A couple of fighter jets flew alongside. They looked like gnats next to a gliding bird of prey. Elon was glued to the sight. The shuttle was traveling faster than the planes but it seemed to hang in the air, like it was being pushed on an invisible hand.

When at last the wheels bumped onto the runway, bounced sulkily, then stayed, Elon had cheered. Parachutes ballooned out from the back of the shuttle, and it seemed to stop in seconds. It stood still, then the astronauts came out.

Elon went back to the book and finished it. The characters decided about Gaia, but they still wanted to find Earth. In the story, Earth was where everything had started. Thousands of planets had people on them, but no one remembered where Earth was anymore. The characters' journey was going to carry on, which meant there would be more books in the series. It made Elon shiver with delight.

He looked down at the street. The lights were bright. Mom, Kimbal, and Tosca would be along soon to pick him up. They'd left him there a few hours ago, but he'd lost all sense of time.

I'm at the start of Mr. Asimov's story, he thought. *I'm at the start of people leaving Earth and exploring the galaxy. I can see the planets of the solar system but only in pictures. I can go into the far distant future to faraway planets in the books I read, but I know that one day it'll be real.*

It was a fantasy like the science fiction books he read, but he wanted to be there when the fantasy became reality. And he promised himself that he would learn everything he could about traveling to space.

He closed the book. It was time to go.

CHAPTER SIX

The Move

Elon thought a lot about his dad. There were a lot of reasons. He really wanted to do something to impress Dad with his computer. He wished he knew better what Dad liked. Also, Dad had started to take him and Kimbal and Tosca on lots of interesting trips. And he had a lot more space of his own at Dad's.

Mostly, though, it was what Grandma kept saying.

"A boy should be with his father, Elon. Especially the eldest boy, like you. Your dad is very sad that you're not with him."

Grandma talked to Elon a lot about what he read and challenged him. Elon had noticed that his dad looked sad, especially when they waved goodbye. It made Elon feel sorry for his dad. And responsible. It didn't seem fair that Dad had no one staying with him.

When he turned eleven, he made up his mind. But he decided to tell Kimbal and Tosca first.

One evening, they were watching *Monkey*. Mom was asleep, exhausted from her two jobs as a diet consultant and model. The three children weren't supposed to watch a lot of TV late, but Elon knew how to work the video so they could watch secretly. They loved the show about gentle Buddha and four animals who had the chance to become human by protecting him. It was hilarious. The fight scenes ruled.

"Unicorn," Elon whispered. "I've been thinking about Dad a lot."

"Unicorn" was Tosca's nickname, which Elon had invented in revenge for her calling him "Genius Boy." She wasn't exactly cool about it, which made it funnier.

"Like *what,* Elon?" Kimbal said, his eyes glued on the TV.

"Don't you think he looks sad? Grandma says he's sad. He misses us."

Neither Kimbal nor Tosca replied.

"Monkey," said onscreen Buddha. "It was greedy of you to eat all that good man's rice." Monkey was always greedy. He looked ashen-faced, disappointed in himself. His lip wobbled.

"Dad looks sad," Elon insisted. "I don't want him to be sad."

Still, the others said nothing.

"I can't help myself," Monkey told Buddha. "It tasted good. How can I put it right?"

"One of us should live with Dad," Elon announced. "I will. Grandma says a son should be with his dad. It'll be fine."

"You have to forgive yourself and ask your friends to help you," Buddha told Monkey.

"Elon, that's crazy!" Kimbal didn't mince words.

"We love Dad," Tosca said in her world-weary voice, "but he makes things too hard. He's always criticizing Mom!"

"I will ask for help," Monkey promised on TV.

"If you do, you will succeed," Buddha replied.

"If one of us saw him more, he'd be different," Elon insisted.

Kimbal shook his head. "He's angry all the time, Elon. Don't you remember?"

"You were four," Elon countered. "How can you know? Anyway, he can change. He can help with school. He can give me opportunities. He'll be happier. It'll make him change."

Kimbal kept shaking his head. "I *do* remember, Elon."

"I can't believe it," Tosca muttered. "It's impossible. Anyway, what'll Mom feel?"

"It'll help her," Elon said stubbornly. "One less of us to look after. It'll give her some time for herself. I'm the oldest. I should do something."

"But ... live with Dad?" Kimbal was still shaking his head in disbelief.

"How bad could it be, guys?" Elon looked between them, willing them to support him.

"Genius Boy hates us," Tosca said with a pout. "I'm going to bed."

She switched the TV off and ran upstairs. Elon watched her, disappointed.

Kimbal twirled the remote in his hands, then turned to his brother. "Are you serious, Elon? It's, like, things are OK the way they are. Why go and do something that hard?"

"To make things better," Elon replied. "Because I can make Dad not be sad."

Kimbal looked sad.

"I shouldn't let you do it on your own," he said after a while. "But then Mom would be so sad."

Elon shook his head. "Let me go first. On my own."

He went through all the same things with Maye a week later. After he'd finished, a haggard look ran across her face. Elon winced. He hated that one way or another, he made someone unhappy. Then Maye put a smile on and sighed.

"You've got a kind heart, Elon," she said. "And a big sense of responsibility. I can't stop you, if it's what you've really decided."

She pulled him close. "But. I love you. Your dad ... he loves you, too. But he ... he likes to be in charge, Elon. He likes things to be his way – and you are very independent. You might not like it. Do you understand?"

Elon remembered exactly what his mom meant.

"He doesn't threaten us, Mom," Elon said. "Not anymore."

"I hope you're right," Maye replied. She sighed again. "You'll always have a loving home with me, Elon, whatever happens."

"I know, Mom," Elon said, hugging her tight. "I love you too. But this'll make everything better. I promise."

The next time the three kids went to their dad's, Elon didn't come home with them. He waved goodbye when Grandma took his brother and sister in her car to Pretoria airport.

Errol Musk put his hand on Elon's shoulder. He was big, dark-haired, and a little chubby. Elon thought it made him proud that his eldest son had decided to move in with him.

They went back home. "Get me a beer," Errol said to a young woman in a white apron. She was the cook. Errol called her Jess, but it wasn't her real name. The woman nodded and came out of the kitchen a minute later with a drink and a glass on a tray. She poured the drink and went back into the kitchen. Errol took a sip.

"Come upstairs, son," Errol said. "I made a new room for you. It's a surprise. I didn't want Kimbal or Tosca to see."

Elon followed his dad. At the end of a corridor, Errol opened a door. The room looked huge. There was a bed, and a model of Grandpa Haldeman's own airplane hung from the ceiling. And there was a computer on the desk. A PC. The most up-to-date model.

"Wow, it's amazing," Elon breathed. "Thanks, Dad."

CHAPTER SEVEN

Dad

Elon soon settled into a routine with his dad. It was much tougher than at his mom's, but he thought it was mostly fine. Grandma still hung out with him. And he had so many more books to read. Often, Dad ignored him, but some days, he focused *so* much on him that it felt like a test. He wanted to know why Elon wasn't perfect in everything in school, and what his projects were, and what he was reading. He had a *lot* of opinions and didn't like to be corrected.

On Elon's twelfth birthday, he showed up in Elon's room before sunrise. He woke him up.

"Time to wake up, son," he said.

"Why? What?" Elon looked at him, half asleep.

"Get out of bed and be ready in fifteen minutes. We have a flight to catch."

"Why?"

"It's your birthday, isn't it?" his dad said. He wasn't smiling. There were no balloons or clowns. No birthday cake. The sun was only beginning to rise.

Dad didn't say where they were going until they buckled into their airplane seats.

"I'm taking you to Cape Town, son," he announced. "We've got a lot of things to do. It's your birthday." He sounded satisfied with himself.

Cape Town was a city on the other side of South Africa. Dad's plan was:

Hike up Table Mountain.

Ride the Cape Point Funicular.

Hit Newlands Stadium for a rugby match between England and Western Province, the local team.

Eat seafood.

Then fly home.

Elon thought it sounded like a pretty crowded birthday trip – and possibly embarrassing. But it could be cool.

Table Mountain towered behind Cape Town, huge and cloud-catching. It had a long large flat top, like its name suggested. From the bottom, it looked like the slope never ended. Dad set a punishing pace. He led the way as if it was a race, through miles of winding paths surrounded by scrub and rock. Every time they passed someone, he grunted happily. It was hard to keep up.

Halfway up, Dad said they would take the cable car down. He started talking about how the cable car worked. Elon stifled a yawn. He already knew about cable cars from the *Encyclopedia Britannica*! Then it got interesting. His dad explained the kinds of steel used to make the fist-thick wires the carriages hung from. He talked about tensile strengths – even went into figures. Elon photographed every word in his mind.

The Cape Point Funicular was just like hiking the mountain, but without having to sweat for miles before the lecture. This time, it was about the difference between funicular and cable railways. A funicular had two carriages, one at the bottom of the run, one at the top. They were connected. As the top one traveled down, it pulled the bottom one up.

"Gravity, Elon, it's just about using the basic forces of nature to our advantage!"

Dad spouted equations excitedly. Elon liked that too.

It was less comfortable when they watched the rugby game. The crowd growled and roared like an earthquake about to strike. Dad joined in like a lion. Elon tried to make sense of the game. The men on the pitch were mostly huge. When they smashed into each other, Elon *saw* the pressure on their bones, like he saw how clouds came together. It was like they were trying to *cheat* the forces of nature.

Dad kept cheering. "Watch that England wing forward, Elon. Peter Winterbotham. He's OK."

When Western Province lost, Dad got upset. They went to a restaurant by the sea in silence. Dad gazed out into the bay. There was an island there called Robben Island. Dad started talking about it.

"You know there's a prison out there, son? You know who they keep there? Terrorists." He spat. "African National Congress terrorists. Nelson Mandela. Have you heard about him?"

Elon nodded. It was evident that his dad didn't like the man.

Elon thought about it. South Africa was a country where only Black people had lived until Dutch and

English settlers came and became the rulers of the land. The government didn't let Black people and White people live in the same places. The Black people couldn't use the same shops or travel on the same buses. They didn't have the rights and privileges White people had. They were the servants. The White people were the masters. It was called *apartheid*. A lot of White people agreed with it, but not all. Some thought it wasn't just, and they fought to change it with their fellow Black neighbors. They wanted equality for everyone, Black and White, but the government persecuted them and put their leaders in jail.

"Maybe, Dad, it's your right to want to fight back if someone takes away your home," Elon said.

"The ANC wants to take ours, son," Dad replied angrily. "You want that?"

Elon decided it was better to talk about funiculars and cable cars. He realized he couldn't change his dad's mind. Later, Dad quizzed him on every single thing he'd lectured about. Elon's photographic memory passed that test easily, but he wasn't sure whether his dad was impressed.

Back home, in Pretoria, his dad took out his rifle and shoved it into Elon's hands. It wasn't loaded.

"When I was your age, I learned to use one of these. You should, too."

Elon lifted the butt of the rifle to his shoulder, looked along the sights, and pretended to pull the trigger. In his mind, the course a bullet would take through the air came as a very clear picture. It flew spinning and broke easily through the target. But he knew how harmful it could be. He handed the gun back to his dad.

"I know how it works, Dad," he said. "Thanks for an amazing birthday. It's been the best ever."

All he wanted was to get back to his room. His father nodded. *At least he isn't upset,* Elon thought.

In his room, he looked at his computer, then took *Foundation* from the shelf and fingered the cover. *Foundation* was about how sometimes things happen in history that were inevitable – just the adding up of lots of small decisions that seemed unavoidable at the time. After a minute, he put it down. He thought about his dad, and about South Africa.

"It's not Dad's fault," he told himself. "He's like that because of where he lives."

He wondered if he would stay in South Africa when he was older and got upset.

Before he went to sleep, he looked at the map that was hanging on the wall.

He found the place.

He knew where he would go when he grew up.

He smiled and fell asleep.

CHAPTER EIGHT

BLASTAR

Elon sat in front of the screen. His eyes had a distant look as he typed line after line of code. In his head, he could see the story of the game he was writing. It was a war of good vs. evil, like *Lord of the Rings*, but in space. He invented the weapons and the sides. The alien attackers got more and more brutal, but if the Earth defenders were fast and used every trick he gave them, they could triumph.

He'd worked on the game for a couple of months, at Dad's and at Mom's. He stored the program on a floppy disk – which was a square of plastic the size of his hand with a disk of metal inside. He was almost ready to show it to Kimbal and his cousin, Russ. But not quite.

He entered the last line of code and took a deep breath.

He had to test the game.

He took the disk out, then slotted it back into his computer's disk drive and waited for the whirring to slow. It reminded him of R2D2, though obviously a billion times simpler. Onscreen, the cursor blinked green. Elon typed in a blur, then the program started.

"BLASTAR."

The screen went blank except for a weird blot at the bottom, like a cross between an arrow and an angry face. Elon's fingers twitched on the direction keys, sending the blot left and right, prowling. Suddenly, meaner-looking arrows appeared randomly at the top of the screen and began to drop.

"So it begins," Elon muttered, getting into character.

He touched the direction key. The blot sped into position. He jabbed. A pixel flew upward into one of the arrows. It blinked out. Elon's blot moved again. Another pixel flew. Another arrow disappeared. The arrows came faster. Elon moved faster. Then a big rectangular bird started advancing down.

"Quick, we need the quasars," Elon announced in an American accent. He stabbed a pattern on the keyboard. This time, a jet of pixels flew up. The bird disintegrated spectacularly, bits of it spraying like rain.

Elon punched the air.

It was a mistake. While his finger was off the keys, one of the arrows sped onto his blot and obliterated it. Game over.

Elon felt angry for a moment, then checked himself. It was OK. The game had to be a challenge.

He played for an hour, then wrote some more code, adding levels.

The following week, he rounded Kimbal and Russ up and locked them in his room.

"This is actively not uncool," Kimbal announced after a minute.

His brother and cousin looked at Elon in awe.

"You know what?" Russ said. "You should send it to the *PC and Office Technology* magazine. They pay 500 rand if they publish your game."

"You think so?" Elon was intrigued. 500 rand was a lot of money, especially for a 12-year-old.

"Dad will find out," Kimbal said, eyes wide. "He doesn't like you just doing games."

"He'll be happy if it makes money," Elon pointed out.

The boys made copies of the game and sent them off, using Mom's address. A few weeks later, an envelope arrived in the mail. It had *PC and Office Technology's* return address on the back.

Elon's hands trembled as he held the envelope.

"They didn't return the disk," Kimbal said, hardly able to hold his excitement in.

Elon opened the envelope.

Inside there was a letter and a check for 500 rand. Elon turned the check over and over in his hands. It was the first time he had earned money from something he'd created. He felt joy. He read the letter again and again. *They really liked it.*

Later, he began thinking about what was next.

He ran his idea by Kimbal.

"Do you think you could sell copies of the game with me?" Elon asked.

"Where?" Kimbal asked.

"At school? You know, after it comes out in the magazine. We could sell at a discount and make more money from the game for ourselves."

Kimbal frowned. "Nice idea, Elon. But I don't go to your school." He still lived with their mom in Durban.

"You *should* though," Elon exclaimed. "Say you want to. It's better than Durban. Imagine what we could do together!"

Kimbal hesitated. "You want me to move in with you at Dad's?"

Elon smiled. "You should move in with me. We'll have the whole week together then. Think of all the things we can do."

Kimbal gave Elon a long look. He didn't like the idea of living with Dad and having to deal with his expectations and bad temper.

But...

Elon could see Kimbal was tempted, so he kept going. "Dad has lots of resources. We can go dirt-biking after school. Or shoot pellet guns. We can build rockets. I mean, whatever we want. I've been researching, actually. I know how to make gunpowder and things. I haven't done it yet, but we could do it together if you came. Dad will be cool with it. He likes practical science."

Kimbal still hesitated. "What about Mom? And Tosca?"

Elon was ready for his brother's question. "Mom will understand. She knows you'll get a better education in Pretoria. Tosca ... well, she'll be better with Mom."

Kimbal still looked doubtful.

"I know what you're thinking," Elon said. "But Dad knows a lot of things it's useful to find out about. And ... well, like, in basic, life is tough, Kimbal. You've got to expect to get hurt and rise above it. You got to learn about that, you know? You'll find out at Dad's. Mom's too easy on us."

Suddenly, Kimbal squared his shoulders. "You're right. It's better to try hard things. But we have to make sure Tosca's OK first, then Mom. Only ask Dad last."

"Sure. Sure." Elon was all eagerness. "That's a good plan. But it'll be OK, Kimbal. It'll be awesome!"

That night, alone, Elon realized how making it a challenge was what had finally persuaded his brother. He thought he should remember that. It was a way you could get people to follow you.

CHAPTER NINE

More Than a Firework

"Elon! Kimbal! Time to go!" Dad's voice ripped upstairs like a bull's.

"We're working on the rocket, Dad!"

"Get down here!"

The two brothers eye-rolled, switched off his computer, and tumbled out of the room.

Dad watched them like a hawk as they put their shoes on. He tapped his watch.

"Ten seconds to get your bikes in the car, or curfew and no dinner," he said. The words were outwardly calm, but the boys knew he absolutely meant them.

They bolted out, Kimbal still holding his trainers, and grabbed their bikes from the garage. Usually, they slalomed around the back garden. Tonight, Dad was taking them to a huge sand track out of town. It had dunes you could use as moguls, and straights pocked with holes. It was brilliant.

They arrived at the car with two seconds to go. The boot was closed. Keys hit the back of Elon's head. Kimbal scrambled them into the lock and threw the door open.

"Eleven seconds," Dad announced, shaking his head.

The boys slumped in disappointment.

"Get in." Dad opened the driver's door. "And next time, don't mess up."

On the way to the dirt track, Dad gave them the third degree about the rocket. According to him, all their design decisions were wrong.

"If you don't work harder, it won't fly," he told them.

Elon screened the insults out, listening hard for any real insights. He decided they weren't doing anything fundamentally insane. He had his own ideas of what they needed to get the rocket right, but they couldn't find anything to make the right size of exhaust shaft. It needed to be a certain size to carry enough fuel to power the rocket really high. They wanted it to go at least two hundred meters up. The design they had so far was too heavy when all the fuel went in, which meant the rocket couldn't get off the ground. But if they experimented...

He ventured that, and Dad grunted. That meant he couldn't think of a criticism – and so Elon was onto something.

The dirt track was in three hundred acres of scraggy bush belonging to one of Dad's business associates. The associate had bought it as a hunting ground for tourists. Legend said there were lions.

"The guy is brain-dead," Dad announced when they arrived. "This place is just a field. Also, he's not tough enough on his employees. Don't ever be soft in business, boys. If you don't control your workers, they'll trick you. Right. Let's see you race."

The two boys pedaled off for the head of the track.

"If you keep being nasty to someone," Elon said when they got there, "they'll *need* to trick you."

Kimbal sniggered.

For the next hour and a half, as the sun sank, they skidded and jumped and straight-lined their bikes at max speed. Sand sprayed like globs of paint. Brakes screeched in unison. They wheelied, one after the other, without even trying, as they accelerated. Elon lost count of how many races they had. It was an even match.

Dad bawled the whole time. "Balance, Kimbal. Elon, don't just show off! Useless, both of you."

They were having fun, but Elon and Kimbal wished Dad would just stop heckling and let them play.

"Curfew," Dad said, jabbing his finger, when they got home. "You missed the target."

They couldn't believe their ears.

"I'll work on explosives," Elon whispered as they went to their rooms.

They felt miserable.

Their dad was away on business for a week after that. In the shed, they lined up their chemicals. Sulfur, saltpeter, and charcoal made gunpowder. A bunch of strong acids and alkalis that combined together would release energy, too. They had brake acid, and some grains Elon smuggled the week before from the water purifier.

"Maybe we should put goggles on," Kimbal observed. They had goggles for pellet gunfights. Elon nodded.

"Let's go."

They came out an hour later, hands burning and faces grimy with soot. Jess screamed at them to wash their hands in lots of running water. It was a good thing, or the acid would have seriously damaged their skin.

But they felt great. They had a formula. The experiments showed them the way. That afternoon, they made the formula up and poured the solution into the two metal cylinders of their rocket. Together, they carried the contraption out of the shed and set it up in the middle of the garden. They had a long fuse because Elon wanted to make sure they could stand a long way back when they lit it. "Live dangerously, carefully!" he said.

And then came the countdown. Ten, nine, eight, all the way to zero. Elon was focused, and his heart beat hard when he lit the lighter.

They watched the spark speed along the fuse and into the fuel chamber. Flames suddenly belched from the bottom. The rocket wobbled, then in an instant flew up into the sky. It sounded just like a jet engine in the distance.

It was so cool!

The two boys cheered like they had scored a World Cup-winning goal. It felt so great. They had accomplished their dream. They had flown a rocket into the sky.

"We have to do that again!" Elon exclaimed.

A few weeks later, at Mom's, they told Tosca.

"How high?" Tosca gabbled. "That is actually almost impressive. I mean, obviously, it's a boy thing and nobody actually needs rockets, but still, if you could get it to paint words in the sky or maybe flowers, it could be cool! What did Dad say?"

Elon gave Kimbal a look. They tried not to laugh.

When they had demonstrated the rocket to him, Dad had just grunted.

It didn't matter. The way Mom smiled when they took out the Instamatic photo prints was just gold. There was one picture of the rocket ready to launch. *Musk's Mars Marauder* was painted on the rocket's side. Then there was the glory shot of the rocket's exhaust fires streaking against the deep blue Pretoria sky.

"You're a good team," she told them. "Just make sure to always take care of each other." She didn't smile when she said those words. She was dead serious.

CHAPTER TEN

"Real" Work

"You boys need to learn about real work," Dad announced, poking his head into the room.

Kimbal and Elon grimaced. They were resting after working on the rocket for school. Elon had three books on the go: *The Hitchhiker's Guide to the Galaxy*, a volume of a new *Encyclopedia Britannica*, and the latest *PC and Office Technology*. He'd recently found out it was better reading several books at once. It gave him more ideas. Dad's gaze fell on the books.

"You *definitely* need to get out into the real world," he said.

He drove them to one of the building sites his company was in charge of. The site stretched in the middle of a forest of high-rises, about the size of a dozen football pitches. It was covered in lots of level concrete squares, like a maze. Walls were going up around the sides of the squares. All had reached different heights.

Hundreds of men climbed ladders and scaffolds or worked on the floors. Most wore ragged t-shirts and denim shorts. They were Black. A few men had short-sleeved shirts and light trousers on, as well as hard hats and walkie-talkies. They were White. The sky above was overcast and sultry.

"Mr. Musk, sir," one of the White men called. "Everything's good here!"

Dad raked his eyes across the whole site without saying anything.

"Come over," he nodded. "My boys here need to learn what it takes to build something real."

They shook the man's hands. His name was Carel du Toit. Dad said he was the site manager.

"Over there," Dad said, pointing. "That block's ready for another story, right?"

Carel looked and nodded. "Lot seventy-eight. Sure, Mr. Musk."

There was no one working on that square.

"Good." Dad checked his watch. "I'm going to the office. When I get back here – at eight pm – I expect that side and the other side to be up. Get your best brickie to teach them, Carel. No one else is to work on it."

Carel blinked. Dad walked off.

The man who came to teach them was called John Moseki. He came from Botswana, a different country. He sent what he earned back to his family.

"How old are you boys?" he asked as he showed them the right grade of sand and cement to mix for a mortar.

"Thirteen," Kimbal said, gesturing at his chest. "He's fourteen."

"Your father is a hard man," John commented.

They didn't disagree.

It went slowly to start with. They had to line up and tamp each brick so it made a perfectly straight line, up and down and sideways. John kept it right with a spirit level. Sometimes, he helped them by putting a whole line of bricks on while they took a break. Carel nodded when he came by.

"Your father will not know," John said.

The day went on, and the wall rose. It wasn't exactly hard on their muscles, but concentrating for hours and having to carry on as it got hotter and steamier made them tired. By the time John stopped for lunch, they just wanted to lie down and go to sleep.

"You boys have something to eat?" John asked as they splayed on the ground.

Elon sat up and shook his head in surprise. John beckoned Carel over and explained. Carel sighed and looked critically at the wall.

"You need to carry on while I send someone out," he told them. "You need to speed up as well. Make sure they do."

He said the last sentence to John, his voice harsher than when he spoke to the boys.

Two bowls of spicy meat stew came. The taste blew Elon's head off, but Kimbal nodded appreciatively. He was into cooking. He wanted to know the spice mix. Both Carel and John shrugged. They didn't know.

The afternoon stretched on. The first and second sides of the wall grew out from the corner, longer and higher. As the sun sank toward the tops of the buildings, Elon and Kimbal found themselves stretching over their heads to lay each new course of bricks. By then, everything ached. But they had their eye in, and John didn't have to correct them so much.

At eight pm on the dot, their dad arrived. They'd managed what he wanted.

"That's real work," he told them as they collapsed into the back of the car.

They would have felt satisfied if they weren't already fast asleep.

The next day, muscles protesting, they played with their pellet guns in the back garden. Moving slowly, stalking, hiding behind jacaranda trees or acacias. Then Elon tried an explosive run, sending a spray of pellets toward Kimbal. Kimbal rolled and shot back. Elon leaned back to dodge and yelped.

"My back!"

They fell down, laughing.

"Yesterday was *so* hard," Kimble said. Elon nodded in agreement.

"You know something?" Elon said. "The work was OK. But do you remember what John said about how the workers, all those Black guys, hardly have enough to eat? And never see their kids? You saw how he had to grovel to Carel all the time. You saw the look in his eyes."

Kimbal nodded. "I hated it, too."

"We should persuade Dad to emigrate," Elon said. "Go to America or something."

Kimbal nodded. But deep in their hearts, they knew Dad would never leave South Africa for another country. Ever. And sure enough, he told them so.

"You think America is better than here?" Dad growled after they made a presentation to him about the bigger opportunities for their education in the United States. "Let me show you something."

He called all their servants – the cook, a housemaid, and the gardener. "Get out of here, and come back after a week," he said. "My boys want to play American."

Jess, Winifred, and Karl looked at each other in bewilderment. "Mr. Musk?"

"You heard what I said."

They left in an hour. Suddenly, the big house felt very empty.

Elon knew what their dad's plan was. He tried not to feel despair.

Dad summoned the two to the living room and waved his hand.

"You make your beds, clean the floors, wash your clothes, look after the garden, cook – all of it. You'll see what life in America is like."

And they did. They cleaned, they made their beds, and they worked the garden.

When they were done, they flopped in bed at the end of a day of housework.

"He really doesn't get it," Kimbal said. Their father wanted to show them how life was easy for them in South Africa with the Blacks – who were treated almost like slaves – looking after them and tending to every whim.

"We'll have to keep trying," Elon replied. "We'll have to find ways to demonstrate that we don't have a future here. We have to."

CHAPTER ELEVEN

The Right Questions

"Elon!" Mom's voice rang up the stairs, followed by Tosca's more piercing echo.

"It's Easter Saturday, Genius Boy. Kimbal's cooked! You have to finish before our cousins get here!"

Alright! Elon thought.

Books were strewn all over his bed. Philosophy, engineering, history, and all his favorite novels. But the book in his hand was *The Hitchhiker's Guide to the Galaxy* by Douglas Adams.

He jumped off the bed, a mischievous look in his eyes. *They'll just have to cope if I think out loud.*

"This is jambalaya," Kimbal announced as they sat down. "I made it with shrimp and added some local greens. It's Cajun – soul food from Louisiana in the United States. It's not exactly Easter Day appropriate, but the ingredients are what looked best in the market."

Kimbal said the last words like they made him king and looked at the three of them eagerly as they forked up the yellow rice mixed with pepper, spring onions, celery, and giant juicy shrimp from the bay. It tasted *so* good, Elon shut his eyes to focus on it. When he opened them, the two boys shared a nod.

"So what's Genius Boy been doing?" Tosca asked. "*Composting* in his bedroom?"

"Thinking," Elon replied, deadpan. "About ... thinking."

"Oh, God!" Tosca eye-rolled.

"OK," Elon went on. "You know Grandma says you have to work-work-work if you want to achieve success?"

"She's right, honey." Mom looked sympathetic.

"OK. But sometimes, it's even better to work smart. Actually, it always is," Elon insisted. "And for that, you have to *stop* working all the time. You need to pause. You have to think. And you have to ask questions. The *right* questions. One in particular."

"Which is?" his mom asked.

"The ultimate question of life, the universe, and everything." He started laughing so hard it looked like his shrimp might fly off from his fork into the wall.

"And what is the answer?" Tosca asked.

"According to the mice and Deep Thought, the supercomputer in this book, the answer is forty-two." He waved the *Hitchhiker's Guide* in the air.

Tosca eye-rolled again. "This is silly," she said.

"It's one of the best books I ever read, and it's hilarious," Elon said. "But at the same time, it makes you think out of the box ..." He smiled and then turned serious. "Maybe it is a silly question," he said. "That's why we need to ask the right questions, not knowing for sure if they are the right questions until we find out."

"I can tell you the right question straight off," Mom said with a smile. "Who's going to wash up? After all, Kimb did all the cooking."

Tosca looked at her plate.

"Me and Tosca?" Elon threw in, digging Tosca in the ribs. "See, answers are obvious when you get the right question!"

Russ, Lyndon, and Peter Rive, Elon's cousins, tumbled into the house just as Elon was drying the last of the pans. Peter was carrying a basket of eggs, painted all different colors and shapes. It wasn't obvious what the shapes were meant to be. They'd had the idea of selling painted eggs all around Mom's neighborhood, as Easter eggs. But only that morning.

Peter placed the basket neatly in one of Tosca's old doll's prams, and they piled out onto the street.

"We should play BLASTAR when we're done," Peter said. He was nine. "With real pellet guns!"

"Maybe," Elon replied. "But I want to talk to Russ and Kimbal first."

They walked up the first drive. The house was a holiday home like Mom's, a bungalow in a small garden of lawn kept green with sprinklers. The sprinklers were on. Peter ran through deliberately and got soaking. A young Black woman opened the door. She looked at them cautiously, then called the owner of the house.

Mrs. Halliday, the owner, was old and frail.

"Easter eggs," Russ said with a wide smile. "Freshly painted. Great for your ... grandkids. Three rand each."

"*Three* for one egg?" the woman said. She picked an egg up and scowled at it, trying to make out what the picture was.

"It's a meerkat," Elon told her. "See how he's standing up on lookout. It's very cute."

"A meerkat, is it?" the woman repeated. "Hmm. If that's what you say." She peered at the six children. "Kaye and Maye's kids. Alright. I don't have my grandchildren with me, but I'll take one for myself."

"You haven't painted them any good," Tosca said as they made their way down the drive. "If they were cuter, we'd sell more."

"You mean if we'd asked what makes people buy a lot of Easter eggs?" Elon teased.

"The right question?" Tosca mocked. "Why didn't you ask it, Genius Boy?"

Elon chuckled. "Because *first,* I have to ask whether getting people to buy Easter eggs is good."

"What?" Russ called out. He was already pushing the pram up the next drive. "We're just trying to make some money. And ... celebrate Easter. How is it not good?"

Elon looked over at Kimbal. "Do you know why our dad's so rich? He mines emeralds. And people *die* in the mines. Black people. So we can have money. I don't think *that's* good. Black people die on his construction sites, too. I asked John. Making money from just anything isn't always right."

Russ stopped the pram and turned around to look.

Elon went on, painfully. "Dad just thinks he should be successful any way he can. It's not his fault. He was brought up that way. But if everyone around him thought differently, he would see that having people die just for him to make money is wrong. Which means ..." He paused. Suddenly, his eyes were alight. "It means ... the only real question is how do you get *more* people to see things as they are and ask the right questions? Collective enlightenment. That's it!"

He felt breathless. He looked at the others.

"So, what about our Easter eggs?" Tosca said, her eyebrows so high they were flying off the top of her head. "What does all this mean for them?"

"No one died to get them," Lyndon offered.

"They're nice for people's little kids," Russ agreed.

"OK. I don't mean we should ditch the Easter eggs." Elon sighed. "But ... it's important. Can't you see?"

"I do," Kimbal said. "You've been wondering what you're meant to do in the world, and now you know."

Elon nodded. Kimbal was right.

Tosca eye-rolled. "We still have to get rid of these eggs. Come on, Genius Boy!"

CHAPTER TWELVE

Live Dangerously, Carefully

Elon and Kimbal swooshed down the mountain, Dad by their side.

"Left ... right ... don't leave off, sons!" he yelled.

They were in the Alps in Europe, on a skiing trip. Dad took them most years, leaving the oven-hot summer in South Africa for snow and the dead of winter.

Every day, Dad tested them in even more difficult snow.

Right then, they were zigzagging down through a forest. As soon as one turn finished, another started. Pine trees zipped past in a blur. Elon kept his eyes glued in front, forcing his legs to keep moving together, first one way, then the other, like his dad had taught him. He was aching with the effort.

Suddenly, Kimbal glided by. Elon gritted his teeth and dared to make his turns smaller and crouch his body lower and further forward. It was the only way to go faster, not by pushing but by letting go and not being afraid of a fall. He found some extra speed and regained the lead.

At the end of the course, the two brothers lifted their ski goggles and bashed each other on the back.

"That was awesome!"

Dad looked at his watch. "You boys are too slow!"

Elon and Kimbal's eyes met. They nodded mischievously.

"Try to catch us!"

Before Dad could speak, they started off again, racing through the queues and snow-covered streets of the village to their cabin. Dad almost overtook them, but not quite.

"Inside!" he ordered, proud but not showing it.

When they finished dinner, he opened a beer and sat down to read the paper. Elon and Kimbal went to their room and called their mom.

"How's skiing?" she asked.

"It's great! We're getting faster. I almost won today!" Kimbal reported.

"That's great, honey," Mom congratulated him. "I'm glad you're having fun!"

"We are, Mom," Elon agreed. "But guess what. When I was going faster and faster and *beating* Kimbal, I couldn't stop thinking about Grandad. It was almost like he was inside my head!"

"Inside your head, honey?" They could hear her surprise.

"Yeah," Elon explained. "Because to ski fast, you have to be risky and skillful at the same time. *He* was like that. It was so cool feeling like him."

"I see. Yes, your Grandpa and Grandma believed in going out and doing what interested them, no matter if other people thought it was crazy. They lived their dreams. And you should, too. But you should always thoroughly understand what you are doing. Live dangerously, carefully. I suppose skiing fast *might* feel like that. They weren't much for skiing, though."

"I *know* that," Elon replied. "Hey, Kimb! Wouldn't it be so cool if Dad let us learn to fly like Grandad!"

Later that night, Elon kept Kimbal awake talking about their mom's parents. He had the very dimmest memory of what they looked like – tall, big-voiced, calm, and kind. Mom was like them. Grandpa used to throw him and Kimbal so far up in the air that it felt like being a rocket. Kimbal didn't remember a thing. He knew what they looked like because he'd seen photographs of them.

Grandpa and Grandma Joshua and Wyn Haldeman, Elon's mom's parents, came to South Africa from Canada. They owned their own small propeller plane, just big enough for two people and their small children. They traveled wherever they wanted to in it, instead of using a car. It didn't go high up, like a passenger jet – just high enough to soar with the birds, free of the ground, yet still able to go to distant countries.

Once, Grandma and Grandpa flew from South Africa to Australia, halfway around the world. It took weeks. They made other long trips to more than sixty countries. Mom said the adventures always felt safe because Grandma and Grandpa thought things through, made plans, and knew how to make new ones if things didn't work out. Planning before they traveled took a lot of time, but it was the most important part of their trips. They were brave. They loved adventure and exploring. And they were good at planning and executing their plans. Elon thought about all the people he knew. His family. His friends' parents. Neighbors. Teachers in school. How many people like Grandma and Grandpa did he know?

None. They were special and had no fear. He wanted to be like them.

"I want to do things like Grandma and Grandpa did, Kimb," Elon announced.

"What? Like be a pilot?" Kimbal said, yawning.

Elon shook his head. "Grandma and Grandpa had a plane because it made sense. They wanted to see exciting places and go where other people didn't. They worked out the *best* way was to learn to fly and own a little plane that could take them wherever they wanted. *That's* the point."

Kimbal grunted. "It was *then*."

"I'm not a copycat, Kimb!" Elon protested. "I'll follow their footsteps, but in a different way."

But Kimbal was already asleep.

Elon tossed and turned. He had to find something that was difficult and worthwhile. But where could he go that was as far away and free as the places Grandpa and Grandma had been to?

I suppose there's space, he thought. *What about seeing another planet? What if I could build a rocket big enough to go all the way to Mars?* He thought about the space shuttle. Mars would be the next stage after taking people to the space station.

"Can I fly on a spaceship? Can I go to distant stars?"

That was a great question!

And the answer was: Why not?

CHAPTER THIRTEEN

Cowhead and Hopeless

The first time Elon ran into Cowhead and Hopeless was when he brought his and Kimbal's rocket to school. The science teacher had agreed he and Kimbal could launch it from the yard – a fenced-off part of the school grounds that was a long way from the buildings. Elon wanted his classmates to see what you could do with patience and by asking the right questions.

There was an impressive crowd from all different years as the Musk boys pulled the pieces of the three-foot-long rocket out of their bags. They lit the fuse. The rocket flared like a million Bunsen burners and roared like a massive motorbike backfiring. It soared up over the school buildings till no one could see it.

The boys cheered as if it was the coolest thing ever. A lot of them came up, high-fiving. Elon and Kimble were happy.

But then the day went wrong. Elon had to pack up on his own because Kimbal had to go straight to class. As Elon walked out of the schoolyard, he passed two boys leaning against the fence. One of them spat as he walked by.

"You didn't make that. It's just a firework. *Bantu* face."

Elon carried on walking. *Bantu* meant black person. It was a racist insult.

The two boys were Cowhead and Hopeless. Names that Elon called them. They looked like little bulls. Blond, tall, chests already wide. On the rugby pitch, they were merciless, and they loved showing off how strong they were.

They were well-known bullies.

When Kimbal heard about it, he was horrified. "You have to sucker-punch them Elon!"

Elon sighed. He knew the bullies were looking for trouble and they had marked him. "Don't worry, Kimb. I won't give in to them. I won't stop being myself. I have to wait."

He meant every word. Hopeless and Cowhead bullied other boys till they joined their gang. But when they picked on Elon, he kept on being himself, which meant, explaining answers with great big smiles and words like "obviously."

"Musk, wipe that smile off your face. You look like a Bantu," Cowhead told him, pulling his ears.

"You are annoying me, and I want to smack you right in the face," Hopeless added.

They were never original. The teachers looked at Elon as if to ask *what are you going to do about it?* They were helpless.

Elon's eyes hardened. "Have you any idea what the perigee of the moon's orbit is, Hopeless?"

Kimbal admired his brother's courage, but it also worried him. The hatred in the bullies' eyes grew every day, like an inkblot. He feared for his brother.

The Kid Who Touched the Stars

It came to a head one day during morning break. Sunlight beat through the tall windows of the second-story corridor of the science building. Elon had a spring in his step. Physics was the next lesson. Physics studied the building blocks of reality. How things actually worked. It was the best lesson. The one where the questions made sense.

Elon approached the stairs down to the physics room. Hopeless and Cowhead were gathered there with half a dozen of their fans. Hopeless saw Elon and looked at the others. His eyes glinted. A smirk played across his face. As if they only had one mind among them all, the boys all moved to block the way.

Elon decided that he could jostle through if he speeded up. He spotted a gap. As he led with his shoulder to get past, Hopeless pushed one of the gang. The gap closed. It was too late to stop, and Elon barrelled on into them all.

"We got you! You are toast!" Cowhead's voice came from the side, just before his elbow speared into Elon's ribs.

Elon lurched and swung his arm instinctively – into Cowhead's jaw. Tears sprang into the bully's eyes, but before Elon could push through, he was surrounded.

Hopeless growled. "Time we teach this Bantu a lesson, boys."

Elon had just enough time to smash his school bag into Hopeless's face before a dozen fists started pounding him. Someone grabbed his arms. Someone kicked the side of his knees. He crashed down on one elbow. It didn't stop. Fists, boots, knees, and elbows slammed into every inch of his body. Somehow, he curled into a ball.

He was still conscious when Cowhead and Hopeless lifted him over their heads and threw him. He heard the gang chanting "Smash Bantu face!" as he flew through the air, legs and arms unfurling helplessly. He crashed into the bottom stair and blanked out.

When he opened his eyes, he saw a blinding light. The pain in his head was excruciating.

He saw his mom, Kimbal, and Tosca. He saw the monitor. His left leg and right arm were in casts.

"Mom, Tosca?" he said faintly. "How are you here?"

"We flew from Durban as soon as we heard," Mom replied, trying hard not to cry. Tosca had tears in her eyes too.

"I'm sorry," Elon said, his voice a croak. Then, wanting to comfort them by making them laugh, he added, "I wish I'd nailed the landing."

"Elon, you have to leave that school!" Mom said.

"I can't, Mom. I can't run away." Elon turned to Kimbal. "How did I get here?"

"Everyone heard the crash," Kimbal said. "Cowhead's gang tried to run off, but they got caught. They were caned in front of the whole school. Cowhead blubbed."

Mom scowled. "Not the greatest way to show that beating people up is wrong."

"Where's Dad?" Elon asked.

Everyone looked at one another. His dad was a no-show in the hospital. "Not here," Kimbal said. "Though he went to Cowhead and Hopeless's families and had a word with their parents."

"What are you going to do, Genius Boy?" Tosca sighed, holding her brother's hand.

"Go back to school," Elon said, closing his eyes. "Show that no one can crush me."

When he got back home, his dad gave him a strange look, angry and sad, like he would boil over. But the only thing he said was, "You better bulk up son."

CHAPTER FOURTEEN

Dungeons and Dragons

Kimbal, Russ, Lyndon, and Peter followed Elon out of the train in Johannesburg. It was a year later, and Elon was fully recovered. He was the leader. The boys all wore t-shirts and jeans and carried backpacks. They wore badges Elon had stamped out of a sheet of metal in Dad's shed. The badges read: *The Dungeon Masters*.

Everyone stalled for a second while Elon checked the map. Then he found a taxi. "Convention center," he said to the driver. The driver nodded and accelerated gently away.

They drew up in front of a long, modern building, ten stories high. A banner hung over the building's lobby saying: *Dungeons and Dragons Convention*. Gaggles of teenage boys were filing under the banner, past bored-looking guards. The guards had guns.

Elon banished his distracting thoughts. The Musks and Rives had come to fight!

He started talking fast.

"We're a team, don't forget. We have a good mix of warriors, wizards, elves, dwarves, and men. We have great weapons and experience. If we're imaginative and take calculated risks, we will *absolutely* win. Live dangerously, carefully!"

He held out his hand, and they high-fived.

They bunched around the reception desk and gave their names. Before long, they had tags on their wrists and were moving through the nests of tables and gangways packed with players.

All five had played Dungeons and Dragons for years. They followed the game's updates and expansions religiously. The newest rulebook was in their backpacks, with packs of new dice of six, four, eight, and twelve sides. Each carried a pad with the characters they were risking in the tournaments. Some were new, others were high-level heroes who had survived many quests and adventures. Each was written on a paper sheet, showing the character's name, strengths, and history. They had spare sheets too, for the Scratch Team Tournament.

First, they had to find the right table. It had a blue flag with the number three. A man was sitting at it. He waved them over when he saw their badges.

"Sit down. I'm Jake. Looks like I'm the *Dungeon Masters'* Dungeon Master!" He waited for them to laugh. The boys cracked a smile.

"Hi Jake, I'm Elon. When do we start?" Elon said, offering his hand.

"They're going to announce it in a sec," Jake said. "Give me your characters. I'll just make sure you comply with the level restrictions and then I'll make copies."

He checked each page as they handed them over. "Nice," he commented. "Good balance. You've got a girl cleric there. Unusual. Made it through a lot, eh? Yes, this is very cleverly done. All legal."

They were allowed five characters, whose total levels added together were a maximum of sixteen. For each characteristic – strength, intelligence, wisdom, and so on – all five characters together could total forty-two. They could have up to five special weapons or spells per character, depending on the character's level. Jake handed their characters back, then a bell dinged, and the tournament began.

The quest was to find the Valley of Lost Souls and rescue a dwarf trapped there by the Lord of Undoing. You had to bring back the dwarf's Soul Ring as well, and if you killed the Lord of Undoing, or stole any of his treasures, you were in for a bonus. Elon liked how it unfolded.

They first went to an inn. Jake described it. Instantly, Elon zeroed in on the signals that someone in the bar was in disguise. He told Peter's wizard to do a secret reveal spell. An orc!

"We'll get him drunk," Elon whispered. "Then interrogate him."

The ploy worked. They were in the Valley of Lost Souls while teams on the other tables were still fighting or trekking uselessly.

All the way through, Elon was steps ahead. His best moment came when everyone thought the adventure was over. Orcs lay piled satisfactorily around the dungeon keep. The dwarf with his Soul Ring was safe, but the Lord of Undoing was nowhere to be found. Elon didn't like it. He really wanted some bonuses. Also, there was something about that dwarf that looked strange. He got Peter to cast another secret reveal spell.

"You see a faint light disappear into Prince Doric's armor," Jake said, poker-faced. Prince Doric was the dwarf's name.

"What's behind the armor?" Elon asked. That was the point of a reveal spell. It showed you the underneath.

"You see a faint light disappear into Prince Doric's armor," Jake repeated.

"The dwarf is not what he seems," Elon announced to the others. He turned to Jake. "I, er, say to him we're glad he's safe, go to clap my hand on his back, but use my dexterity to sink my Assassin's Carver in his neck."

"You want to kill Prince Doric!" Jake challenged.

"Roll the die," Elon told him, grinning.

It was the eight-sided die. Elon's character got plus three on any throw because of his dexterity. He won.

"As your knife sinks in, it melts," Jake told him, quietly. "And at the same time, Prince Doric disappears. Instead, you see a shadow of swirling air in the shape of a person."

"The Lord of Undoing," Kimbal said loudly. "We have to kill him!"

They could hardly contain their excitement. Elon gestured to keep their voices down so the other tables couldn't hear.

The fight lasted minutes. The evil lord killed Elon's assassin and Russ's girl cleric, but in the end, Kimbal and Lyndon's warriors and Peter's wizard prevailed.

No one on the other tables spotted the trick.

"We won the tournament, Dad," Elon announced when they got back home.

"Winning's a good habit. Do it in the real world," his dad said.

Elon didn't say anything. He was still excited. And no one could change the way he felt. He was a winner. They had won, and it felt amazing.

Elon tossed and turned in bed that night. His dad's words bothered him.

"Dad's right," he told Kimbal the next morning. "I love D&D, but we have to win in the real world, too."

CHAPTER FIFTEEN

Cars or Mars?

"We have to change everything to solar power. Really, it needs to happen *now*."

Elon lounged back from his desk. He was in geography, at the Boys High school in Pretoria. He was nearly sixteen. The class was discussing how South Africa got its electricity.

The boy sitting behind Elon looped his finger by his temple. The class sniggered.

"That's... unlikely," the teacher told Elon.

Elon shook his head. "The technology is not that hard. Especially somewhere with South Africa's weather!"

The teacher wanted to know more.

"You know, it's easy to build pipes that you can run water through and get the sun to heat the water in the pipes. It gets hot enough for washing, drinking, cooking, everything. Even better, the science for converting sunlight to electricity is really well known. It's just a manufacturing challenge."

He gazed around the mocking faces filling the room and continued. "Oil is just some lakes in the ground that will be empty soon. Coal, too. Besides, the fumes from smoke are pure poison. And there's this thing called the greenhouse effect. You know about that?"

Their eyes were glazing over. "The more we burn, the hotter it gets," Elon continued. "Boom! Within our lifetime, no crops, not enough water. Death and destruction."

He waited for his teacher's response.

The teacher looked uncomfortable. Elon would bet his life that the man did less reading than him about how the climate worked. For Elon, it was the latest development. He had worked out a really *important* question. It was the same as the one in the *Dune* and *Foundation* books. What if humanity can't survive? He had done research on whether there were real threats. It turned out there were. And they were really real!

"This is a complicated question, Elon," the teacher said. "Mining creates a lot of jobs. Also, there are other ways of producing energy. Class?"

"Nuclear power?" someone offered.

Elon almost exploded. "Does no one watch the news? Chernobyl, anyone? No. Solar power is the power of the sun – it's safe and clean and has no end."

"What about cars?" a boy jeered. "Since when can *they* go on sunlight?"

"Actually the first cars to be sold were electric," Elon pinged back. "Morrison Electric in 1891. And Porsche P1 in 1898. So the answer is easy. Use rechargeable batteries. Charge the batteries with electricity you create by using the sun's energy."

"The problem is Bantus," drawled a bored voice at the back of the room. "They breed too much. Stop them having so many children. This country won't need so much electricity then."

Elon felt the blood drain from his face.

"Apartheid won't survive," he muttered between his teeth. "It's obvious."

The boy at the back ground his teeth in return.

Elon looked him in the eye. The boy wouldn't dare attack him. Elon had bulked up at last and was taking martial arts classes. A punch from him meant something. But he wanted to persuade people, not beat them up.

"We're not discussing politics," the teacher said, stopping everything. "Class. Write an essay. 500 words. Topic: pros and cons of alternatives for oil and coal in *today's* Africa."

He looked straight at Elon as he stressed the word *today*. At the back, the racist leered and flicked Elon the finger.

"We actually do need people to settle on Mars as well," Elon told Kimbal when they were walking home from school. "Because the more you think about it, the more it's obvious the human race needs another home planet."

"Is that for real, Elon?" Kimbal teased.

"Everyone knows how dinosaurs went extinct," Elon replied. "Big comet, massive explosion, the Earth went into such a deep winter for so long hardly any life survived. It could happen again. Having a second planet is like a safety net. Like backing up your data!"

Kimbal laughed.

"You know what, Kimb? I think about Dad as well," Elon said. "Everything he knows about mining and building, it would just be so good if he was up on Mars. Someone like him could actually do it. You could put him to good use instead of just digging up jewels."

"Or what about you?" Kimbal asked. "Why couldn't you? You're Genius Boy, after all."

"I'm fifteen," Elon deadpanned.

"Your life is ahead of you!" Kimbal teased. "That could be your ambition."

Elon thought for a moment. "But I can't decide what's most needed. Mars or sun-powered electric cars!" He got his faraway look. "Kimbal, it won't happen unless someone with a very large amount of money decides to do it. So the big question is not solving the engineering, it's solving the money."

He bunched his fist and punched his hand. "I have to work out how to make money and save humanity doing it."

They began laughing.

"And *I* have to work out how to save people by cooking the greatest food," Kimbal said suddenly. "You know that's going to be essential, too!"

Elon pricked up his ears. Kimbal told him about his own research, that a lot of farming used too many chemicals to be healthy and how the soil was being washed away all over the world.

"Food, electricity, space," Elon repeated. "We have to do something about all of them."

They laughed again.

"Know what? We have to get into practice," Kimbal said. "We have to get ready for when we can leave and do our own thing."

"Let's show everyone what a Musk can do," Elon cheered. "Let's make a ton of money!" He went comically silent. "But how?"

CHAPTER SIXTEEN

Hustle

"We can absolutely do this," Elon told Kimbal.

The two boys were sitting in front of Elon's Apple Mac in Dad's house. A document was open, headed with the words "MUSK-A-RAMA" and a photo of a pinball machine.

"We better keep who we are top secret," Kimbal said. He scribbled notes on a blank pad as he spoke. "Ring around suppliers. Get a good discount for bulk purchases. Scout out sites. Drive a hard bargain with landlords who are basically a bunch of leeches anyway so they deserve it. Draw up a really great marketing campaign."

"And get a bank loan and a permit," Elon added.

"Oh yeah, a permit."

They looked at each other, silent for a second.

On Kimbal's pad was a drawing of a room with pinball machines lining three walls, and two t-shirted young men sitting at a cash desk. That was their idea for practicing making money. But they faced a real challenge: you needed permission from the local council to run a pinball arcade. And you needed money to pay for all the equipment at the beginning.

"People love pinball," Elon said firmly.

"They don't *have* to know you're sixteen and I'm fifteen," Kimbal observed, equally firmly.

The Kid Who Touched the Stars

They looked at each other again.

"Everyone will want in," Elon continued. "Dad ... Mom ... Grandma .... As soon as they see we have actual pinball machines lined up and an actual space."

"Uncle Scott," Kimbal suggested.

"Headmaster!" Elon played his trump card. "The bank will love us."

They nodded, feeling pumped up.

"Let's get started!" they chorused.

They ran downstairs and shot out of the house before Dad could ask what they were up to. Could they really pass themselves off as young men, not the schoolboys they actually were?

Elon was confident. "*I've* got all the facts and figures and I've got Mom's smile and I've listened to Dad's friends floating business ideas at each other. I can do the talking."

"Guys our age *are* the guys who love pinball. We really *do* understand the customer base," Kimbal said.

"But *you* talk to people better," Elon went on. "I hate to admit that, but you do."

"We both have strengths," Kimbal reassured him. "We'll double-team it."

It took a whole month before the crunch came and they needed to reveal their ages. It was a lot of fun.

First, they looked for a space. They skidded down dusky, seedy streets on their bikes, and crisscrossed the city on the bus looking for the right place. Estate agents looked at them in disbelief when they first saw the backpacks and Elon's baby face. But then he wove a spell with his vision for the arcade. Kimbal came in when the agents started talking money.

"Look at the wall. It's peeling! We need a better window frame. This backroom leaks like a sieve," he said, trying to negotiate the best price.

Then it was about finding the best pinball machines.

Acting the skeptic with the pinball machine makers was even more fun than with estate agents. The two boys would turn up and give each other weary looks. Then they peeled off with their backs to each other and got the machines ringing like a Strawberry Switchblade song. Afterward, they rolled their eyes softly at the sales guys.

"Those machines have terrible balance."

"That win ratio? How can anyone make money with that?"

They brought Russ in as possible staff, as well as a couple of Kimbal's friends from school.

They filled in every form for the permit.

And at last, they showed up at the bank.

Mr. de Klerk, the bank manager, went wordlessly through their business plan while they sat opposite his desk. When he finished, he leaned back, steepling his fingers.

"Errol Musk's boys, is that correct?" he asked.

Kimbal nodded. Elon just stared.

"I wouldn't expect anything less than a cast-iron business plan from Errol's sons," Mr. de Klerk continued. "*I'd* back you. But you obviously know someone over eighteen has to sign your contracts. *And* your application for a permit."

Elon nodded.

Mr. de Klerk's eyes twinkled. "Who've you got?"

"Would *you*, Mr. de Klerk?" Elon dared to ask. "You say it's a good plan."

Mr. de Klerk nodded slowly. "I see. You hustle well. So go and hustle your dad."

"He doesn't necessarily *mean* Dad," Kimbal said as they approached their front door. "We have other options."

"They'll all ask what Dad thinks," Elon said, looking several steps ahead. "We'll just have to go for the jugular!"

"Don't waste my time!" Dad roared, besides calling them stupid, lazy, and no better than a pair of Bantus. "Do you want to waste your lives?"

"Of course not, Dad," Elon countered. "It's just a quick dodge. It's just for before we go to America."

Dad froze.

"No son of mine will get involved in gambling," he said at last. "Don't let me hear about this again."

Then, as if the words were stones he was mining from inside himself, he continued. "Also, I expect you back here if you ever get degrees in America. This country needs boys like you."

They spent the weekend at Mom's, and they talked about it with her.

"I would have worried the same," she told them. "Think of the distraction. You have to graduate if you want to follow all your dreams. Make a plan. Don't just fritter your time away."

"It was a plan," Elon muttered. "It just had one flaw."

"What I don't understand," Tosca said, "is why you thought it was OK to make money from gambling. How does that match up with asking the right question?"

Elon had no answer for that.

CHAPTER SEVENTEEN

No Way Out

Elon and Kimbal's eyes locked onto the AK47 assault rifle. Seeing it was the kind of thing you came across on the Pretoria–Jo'burg line.

The gun was slung across a Zulu girl's middle, loose and low enough to aim and fire in a single second. She hung off the side of the carriage for Blacks, part of a line of young men and women doing the same. Maybe they hadn't found space inside. Maybe they couldn't afford a ticket. She wore shorts and a frayed Free Nelson Mandela t-shirt, as good as a sign over her head saying ANC: African National Congress. Dad would call her a terrorist. Others would call her a freedom fighter. She looked Elon's age. The two boys gawped in admiration at her out of their window in the Whites' carriage.

Once in a while, her eye caught theirs. Elon wished he could make his face look cool and like he respected the girl, but he just wore a super embarrassing goofy smile. Her lips curled, kind of amused, kind of with contempt.

Abruptly, she trained the muzzle directly at them, single-handed, finger hooked steady as a rock around the trigger. Her expression became a mask of cold hatred. Elon and Kimbal's jaws dropped. They were afraid and unable to take their eyes away.

Just as suddenly, she sprang away from the train. So did all the other hangers-on. It was just before the next station and time for them to get off. The girl landed in the dust by the track and ran a few paces to keep her balance. The whole time, she kept Elon and Kimbal squarely in her machine-gun's sights. The train slowed down and began to leave her behind. She turned the gun's muzzle to keep it aimed.

Finally, she burst out laughing, winked, and shouted something at them in her own language. Then she twirled the barrel onto her shoulder and disappeared into the scrum of people. They siphoned off between the buildings in front of the station.

"Oh my god," Elon breathed, leaning back into his seat. Kimbal was stunned and white as a sheet.

They giggled for a couple of seconds in relief.

"Won't you miss that?" Kimbal said.

"Are you kidding?" Elon shot back. "We need to get out of this place. Once we're out, we can do something actually interesting and useful with our lives." His heart was still racing. "Here is insane, Kimbal, and it might get worse. We have to go to America *soon*."

Kimble nodded. "This country is a prison to so many people. And for you and me. Not because of the color of our skin, but because we can't fulfill our dreams here. Especially you, my bro."

"I want to study at a great college in the United States," Elon said. "Then I want to go to Silicon Valley."

Silicon Valley was a dream for Elon – a place where all the big minds were working on big ideas and making them happen.

"How is that going to happen?" Kimbal pulled a face. "Dad expects us to do our army service, get a South African degree, then have our adventure, then come back."

Elon shrugged. "No. We should do college in the United States, skip the army, skip university here. Definitely not ever come back."

"OK, Genius," Kimbal said with a laugh. "But remember what Mom's friend said? You don't get out of high school without Afrikaans, and yours is like the suckiest in the whole wide world. If you can't graduate from high school, you can't get to college in America."

Now Elon pulled a face. "Afrikaans is a waste of headspace."

"So learn enough to pass and then delete, dimwit." Kimbal flicked his forehead. "Come on Elon. If you have a plan, you have to do all the steps to make it happen."

Elon was annoyed. Afrikaans was what most of the Whites spoke, but it was useless in any other country in the world. He didn't understand why he should have to obey a stupid rule when it was obvious his future was somewhere else. *Because if he didn't toe the line, he couldn't get to study what he ought to.* Blah-blah. It made him angry.

"We can't go directly to the United States," he said. "We need first to get a Canadian passport. Then we can go to college in America and work on our US citizenship."

"Mom," Kimbal said.

"Yes. But there is a bit of a problem," Elon said. Maye was born in Canada and she was a Canadian citizen, but her kids were born in South Africa.

"So what do we do?" Kimble grumbled.

"I don't know," Elon said.

A couple of months later, Elon sat in a burger joint near Pretoria Boys High school. It was lunchtime. He had just aced an Afrikaans test, but he still felt frustrated. Kimbal and he had lots of ideas about making the world better, but they could do nothing to make them real.

He looked at the jacaranda trees outside. It was coming into summer, and the blossoms hung off the trees like perfumed purple silks. He remembered Mom's story about seeing them when she first came to South Africa from Canada.

He didn't have a way out yet. *I really don't want to go into the army, and I really don't want to have to defend apartheid. I want to be free in a free country and live my dream.*

The only way to postpone the army was to enroll in the University of Pretoria. While he was there, he would find a way.

But time was running out.

CHAPTER EIGHTEEN

Freedom

You could hear Elon's shout of joy from the other side of Durban. He calmed down enough to snatch the letter from his mom's hands and read it through himself. Too good to be true. But it *was* true!

"They really did it, Mom," he shouted when he finished. "They really changed the rules!"

Another roar of joy.

"It looks like they did." Mom sounded unruffled, but the way she smiled said it all. She, too, was alight with relief and hope.

"We can all go?" Tosca said. "We can all become Canadians?"

"That's what it says," her mom confirmed. "If you have a Canadian parent, you now have an automatic right to live in Canada."

Elon paused, already thinking practically. "OK. I have to get the documents done."

"It'll take some time," Mom said.

She ruffled Elon's hair. He shook his head, getting her off. "OK. So first, I'll go to the embassy in Pretoria. That's quickest."

Mom winced. "We have to go together, Elon. It all depends on me proving myself to them. *I* have a lot to do before *you* can get involved." She smiled. "For once, you'll have to be patient."

"That's right Mr. Make-it-all-happen-yesterday," Tosca teased.

Elon didn't like it one bit. He was sixteen! Why should he still have to wait for his mom? Even if it was his own mom?

"I need to work out a plan," he announced, grabbing his jacket and making for the door.

"Hey, wait for me!" Kimbal protested.

"I can't," Elon insisted.

He was gone before Kimbal got on his shoes. He practically ran down the street. It was because the idea forming in his head couldn't include Kimbal. The minute he read the letter, he knew he couldn't wait for his brother to graduate from high school. It would take a year, and by then, he would have to do his army service.

He knew what he'd do. *Basically*, he decided, *I should fly to Canada the same day I get my citizenship*. He mapped it out in his head. He could hook up with relatives, work whatever jobs it took, get into a good university. He would have to check what the fees were. But he decided that if he had to, he would work all through university to pay the fees. Then, even Dad couldn't stop him.

He came to a crossroads, panting hard with excitement. For the first time in his life, a clear way to freedom had opened up in front of him. He plunged forward, walking as fast as he could, farther and farther from home.

Just think of what I can do with freedom. He had no fear. He was a teenager, and kids his age weren't supposed to fly to the other side of the world with no money and start a new life with no adult to take care of them. But he knew deep in his heart that he would be OK. He was confident because he had a plan and thought he could see all the risks. He thought about the worst-case scenario: his dad showing up and grabbing him by the collar to take him back home. He could easily risk that!

CHAPTER NINETEEN

No Turning Back!

Nearly a year passed by. Elon couldn't believe how long it took! Every week, it seemed there was another thing to do.

They didn't just visit the embassy. They had to write and wait for replies to come through the door, then write replies to the replies. The embassy had to send some of the letters back to Canada for the officials there to read. They also had to get lawyers to sign copies of Mom's birth certificate and passport, and all the children's, too.

At last, they made a final trip to the embassy. They all stood together, made a promise to be true citizens of Canada, and sang the national anthem, including in French! Elon wanted to swear on the *Hitchhiker's Guide* because he said it was his Holy Book. Mom told him not to. "They might not appreciate your line of humor as much as others," she said.

When all was said and done and the passport arrived in the mail, it was time to buy tickets. But before all that, he had to tell Dad what he was going to do.

"You'll come creeping back here inside *one month*. When that happens, don't expect any respect from *me*!" Dad was standing by the barbecue, turning steaks over it at the same time as he shouted.

Elon had just explained he was leaving South Africa and never coming back. While his dad ranted, Elon looked up at the sun beating out of the endless blue sky, and the dazzling green of the lawn. It wasn't streaked with dust anymore, not like when Kimbal and he used to race around it on their bikes.

"I won't come back," he insisted. "I won't need to. You taught me a lot of skills, Dad. I will easily find work."

Dad wouldn't have it. "Where will you stay, son? In some dirty room full of rats? Is that what you want?"

"Mom has relatives," Elon countered. "I'll start with my great uncle in Montreal. It really won't be a problem, Dad."

Dad stewed on it for a moment, then spat. "You're a traitor. A coward. The Bantus are fighting us, but you won't stay to build your country. You're just scared to fight in the army. You're weak."

"Actually, I hate apartheid, Dad," Elon argued, feeling angry himself. "Plus, how will I ever learn anything about computer science or physics here? Everyone's too busy killing one another."

"This country belongs to *us*," Dad retorted. He was breathing heavily. "You aren't strong enough to keep what's yours. That's why you'll fail. Trust me."

Elon didn't bother arguing anymore. He knew Dad was wrong about him.

He held his Dad's gaze, and changed the conversation to his dad's favorite sport. "Western Province aced the game last night."

Dad turned his back. "Bulls' defense was useless. No backbone at all." He shrugged. "Even you could have broken them."

Elon laughed hollowly. In his mind, his eyes were fixed on the calendar. He counted the days down to when he wouldn't have to listen to any insults like that ever again.

The morning Elon left South Africa, the airport was buzzing. Mom, Tosca, and Kimbal clustered around him, looking proud. His suitcase was already on the plane.

"It's time," he said, feeling impatient. He hugged them one by one.

"See you soon, Genius Boy!" Tosca sniffled.

"Follow me quickly," Elon whispered to Kimbal.

As the 747 climbed, Elon watched the dusty city shrink till it looked like a toy. His heart felt huge.

When they landed in Montreal, he handed over his Canadian passport, and the official gave him a friendly nod. "Welcome home," he said.

Elon smiled and went to collect his suitcase, feeling elated.

Out in the arrivals area, he paused.

Now what? For a moment, he felt lonely.

He found a payphone and gave the operator his great uncle's name. He waited, a little excited, a little afraid. The operator came back on the line.

"I'm sorry, but there isn't anyone of that name in the directory," she told him. "Can I help you with another number?"

Elon couldn't believe it. Then the memory of his dad's words came back. He ground his teeth with determination. He dialed Mom in Durban.

He could hear her relief when she heard him. "Honey, you know I wrote your uncle. Well, I just got his reply. He moved to *America*. To Minnesota." She paused and then came up with a suggestion. "I'm sorry. You must be tired from the long flight. But you can easily stay in a youth hostel."

Rapidly, Elon recalculated his whole plan. "OK. Good. Thanks, Mom. I guess I'll look around Montreal for a couple of days. Then I can check out other family members. Can you get their numbers for me? I'll call again tomorrow."

The thing about Mom, he told himself, *is she makes you feel safe, even when she might be scared.*

The next day, he walked around the city. It was cloudy and nowhere looked dusty or dry. The trees along the roads looked like people hadn't planted them there, like the remains of old forests. No one stood guard outside the shops. He looked around the computer shops and the new technology. Then he investigated the railways and the buses. To his delight, he discovered that for just $100, he could get a bus ticket to travel anywhere in Canada.

That meant he wasn't daunted when he got Mom's list of relatives. He checked the map of Canada to see where he should be heading.

Saskatchewan? You are kidding me. He laughed to himself. *That's on the other side of the country. Thank God for that bus ticket.*

Live dangerously, carefully. And some. He was determined not to look back.

CHAPTER TWENTY

O Canada

Elon stood in a timber mill boiler room, wearing giant white overalls, clutching a helmet. It was a hazmat suit, designed to protect his whole body and keep his lungs safe. In front of him was a hole just about big enough to wriggle through. Another man, dressed just like him, poked his head out of it. Elon reached for the guy's shoulders and dragged.

Once he was through, the guy took off his helmet, gasping.

"All yours, buddy!"

Elon high-fived the man, then plunged past down the hole.

He was in his third week working in the timber mill. Hauling his body into the boiler chamber was the easy part. Through the hole was a dingy bunker room made of concrete and metal. The boiler that kept the mechanical saw going was in there. It rattled and shook with a whine like a jet engine warming up. Sawdust swirled in piles on the floor.

Elon had to grab the shovel that was always left in the room and dig it into the piles of dust. Then, with a swing, he had to empty the shovel down the hole he'd just wriggled through. If he didn't, the dust might catch fire and the whole sawmill would burn down.

As soon as he stood up next to the boiler, water ran off him inside the suit. It was like he was plunging under a hot water tap. With a grunt, he thrust the shovel down into the sawdust, lifted it, and threw the dust down the hole. Thrust and throw. Thrust and throw. After half an hour, he had to crawl back and let the next guy take his place.

They were only allowed half an hour in there. Any longer would get you so hot you might faint or, worse, even die.

Elon didn't mind how hard it was at all. It was an important job, right in the heart of the machine. It paid eighteen dollars an hour, enough for him to give the cousins he was living with some money for rent and still save a lot. That made him feel great. He felt like he was becoming a man in his own right. His muscles bloomed, and the muscles in his mind too. He thought about the hopes and fears of the other workers. He learned how to stay completely alert, even in a stressful situation.

He dragged himself down the hole after his half hour. The supervisor was waiting when he came out. He took off his helmet and nodded, breath blowing hard.

"Great work rate, buddy," the supervisor said. "Seems like nothing ever makes you stop!"

"I've got my target," Elon puffed. "It doesn't make sense to me to go for less than my absolute maximum."

"Make sure you pace yourself, my friend," the supervisor said. "I can't have you falling over on me!"

The Kid Who Touched the Stars

"I have a good sense of my limits," Elon replied. "I really do. I know what my reserves are."

The supervisor clapped him on the back. "I hope so. How long do I get to keep a going-places man like you?"

Elon scooped up the sawdust that was now coming out of the hole and started filling a barrow.

"My brother comes over from South Africa in a month," he said with a smile. "We're going to look for universities together."

"Good luck with that," the supervisor said. "See ya in the canteen."

Elon nodded and smiled.

When Kimbal arrived, the two brothers remembered their time trying to set up a pinball business and decided it would be fun to hustle again. They thought that, in the year before studying, they should get as varied an experience as possible.

"We should meet people who run corporations," Elon said. "If we get to know them, we can learn from them. Maybe we could do business with them one day."

Kimbal frowned. "How will we get to meet CEOs?"

"Find their phone numbers and call them up!" Elon said.

"It won't be hard."

It was like a game of dare. Each brother picked a person that sounded interesting and called them up to get a meeting. They took turns. Elon kept a score of how many meetings each of them managed to set up. When someone agreed, they really turned on the charm.

"That guy," Kimbal said, jabbing his finger at the business directory. "He's CEO of a major bank. If we meet him, we could discuss your making money to engineer electric cars ideas!"

"He *is* a good one," Elon agreed. "But her, too," He pointed to another name. "She's in charge of logistics at a trucking company. We could find out so much about what gets moved around and from where and to who. If I ever make electric cars, I need to know how that happens."

"We had this idea," Elon told the bank CEO, who did agree to meet them, "of using computers to make it easier to pay money. You would have a file on your bank's computers for each customer. The customer could get into it with a password. They could send payments to other people. Like with making a payment by telephone. It would be so much cheaper for the bank."

"You need someone to write the program to do it," Kimbal chimed in. "There are lots of young people, like us, who would love to do that."

The CEO laughed sympathetically. "I can see you would!"

He leaned across the big mahogany meeting room table in his office high above the city in Toronto. "But let me give you a little advice." He put a finger to his lips. "Most big banks like us don't really like doing anything new. I like the way you think. But you might have to write that program yourself and start your own bank. Could you do that?"

"Why not?" Elon nodded. "Once I own a bank, I can fund all the other things I want to do!"

All three of them laughed.

But as Elon and Kimbal walked away from the glass tower of the bank headquarters, Elon had that old faraway look in his eyes.

Make a fortune from a new computer-based bank ... find the right group of engineers ... build electric cars ... and build new rockets that could send people to Mars.

It sounded like a plan!

"What's for lunch?" Kimble asked. He was always down to earth.

They agreed on burgers and fries.

CHAPTER TWENTY-ONE

Ice Cream for Two

Dear Elon, the note read. *I have an exam tomorrow and I have to study. I'm so sorry I have to cancel our ice cream date. Justine*

The note was pinned to Justine's door. Elon picked it off slowly and read it again. He stood for a minute, tapping his foot. Then he pocketed the note carefully and made off down the corridor.

Elon was two weeks into his first year at Queen's University in Ontario. Justine was a black belt in Taekwondo and the most intelligent and beautiful woman he had ever met. He'd run into her at a freshman party. His first words were "Hi, I'm Elon, I think a lot about electric cars."

It sounded ridiculous. But then Elon explained that he was practical, and it was an environmental concern. She realized he knew what he was talking about and stayed.

"I'm interested in abnormal psychology," she told him. She explained it so well that he decided he wanted to study it himself.

He read the note again and then got back to his room. It was full of computer parts, computers that were opened up and being repaired, and computers he was building. He did it for fellow students. It made him friends as well as money.

"You know Justine Wilson?" he asked his roommate. "Can you remember her friend's name? We met her at the freshman party."

His roommate was from Hong Kong, and he was the most conscientious student Elon had ever met. He smiled up at Elon.

"Is it the girl you were talking to with Farooq? I didn't meet her."

"But Farooq did?" Elon pressed.

"Yes. If it *is* that girl."

Elon pursed his lips and turned to go out.

"Wait," his roommate called. "Do you want these lecture notes? Shall I put them on your bed?"

Elon's face brightened. "Thanks. I'll get them back to you later."

He set off again, fast.

As he searched for his new friend Farooq, his mind churned. A dozen different conversations went on inside him.

He thought about his physics classes. They were working through the results from the newest experiments about the inside of atoms. The room was full of people who were really into it, like him. He wasn't the only one asking questions and wanting to test what was really true. He remembered the same in his economics class. It was like having fifty Kimbals to talk to.

One guy challenged his ideas about how to make rechargeable batteries. Another told him about some metal mixtures that could make lighter and stronger rocket tanks. Some people shared his ideas that the World Wide Web would make banks obsolete.

It was like being allowed to take all your favorite animals home from the zoo.

He got so absorbed that Farooq saw him first.

"Hey, Elon! Where are you going so fast?"

Elon's reply came in jabs. "Justine Wilson's friend? What was her name?"

Farooq laughed and told him. "But I thought it was Justine you liked!"

"I do!" Elon shouted as he hurried off.

Christie. Her name was Christie. He muttered.

Suddenly he saw her. "Hey! Christie!" He ran up to her. "Christie. Hi. Sorry."

"Elon?" She smiled.

He paused for breath. "I wondered … if you could tell me … where Justine … is."

"What is this about, Elon?" Christie asked. She looked at him like he was a specimen, but not a bad one.

"Oh, I …" Elon hesitated. "I wanted to ask her about abnormal psychology again. Is she about?"

"Right." Christie gave him a look. "I guess she'll be in the language library. She has a Spanish exam, you know?"

"Sure, yeah." Elon nodded. "You know, I bet she wishes there was a way to just take in food and not have to interrupt what she's doing. Like some kind of pill. I do! I hate to slow my productivity!"

Christie laughed. "This is about that ice cream date, isn't it? She's really sorry. But she really does have an exam!"

Elon nodded. "I think I *can* still buy her ice cream. It's almost a perfect studying food. Spoon the ice cream in with one hand and turn the page with the other. Don't you think?" He gave Christie a shrewd look. "Do you know what flavor she likes?"

"Elon Musk!" Christie tutted. Then she smiled. "I guess that isn't a horrible idea. Triple chocolate, obviously. Isn't that everybody's?"

"Thank you." Elon flashed a big charming smile. "I like you."

"Don't forget she has to study!" Christie called after him.

Elon loved the library. It was modern, with long windows letting in floods of light over the neat, close stacks of books. The glow invited you and made you long to open your mind. It reminded him of the old bookshop in South Africa. He felt at home.

He walked down the bright central aisle, his gaze traveling right and left. Two triple chocolate ice creams gleamed in his hands.

Justine was next to a window. Open books covered her table. Her long hair was tied back, and her face was knotted in concentration. He walked up to her.

"Justine?" he began. "Hi. I thought you might like …"

She started. "Oh my god! Elon!"

"... Ice cream." He held a cone out toward her.

She blinked, then focused.

"Triple chocolate?" she said in wonder. "Thank you so much. How did you know?"

She took a lick, and a contented look spread across her face.

"Obviously, you're studying," Elon said. "But I figured you could do that while you're eating. Abnormal psychology. Do you think it's abnormal to *see* complex processes – logical thoughts, in your mind? In, kind of, three dimensions?"

Justine's eyes clouded as she considered this. "Gosh, I don't know Elon. I don't think abnormal is the word I would use for that. It sounds more like some kind of physical thing, like how sounds have colors for some people. Why?"

"Things come through visually for me," he admitted.

"That is so interesting," she replied. "Maybe you should get studied."

He laughed out loud. She shushed him with her eyes.

"It's a very useful strength," he added.

"I'll bet!"

He licked his ice cream and smiled. *It's a good start,* he thought.

New Frontier

It was November 16th, 2020. Elon Musk, owner of Tesla electric cars and SpaceX rockets, drove his Roadster into the Cape Canaveral launch area. It was a nail-biting day. His Falcon Full Thrust rocket was sending people into space for the first time. Two astronauts were going aboard, in the Dragon space capsule. They were flying to the International Space Station.

Elon steered the electric sports car to the giant lift by the launchpad. Video crews and journalists buzzed around it. Elon was going there for a photoshoot with the two astronauts. As the storm of flashlights went off, he waved. The astronauts disappeared into the lift. Elon gave a fist pump, then jumped back into the Roadster and headed to mission control.

On some days, Elon was now the richest man in the world. The money came in from building electric cars at Tesla and launching satellites into space with SpaceX. And it had all begun with inventing a new kind of online financial institution, PayPal, just as he'd imagined years ago when he was hustling with Kimbal during his first year in Canada. If it wasn't true, you would say it was crazy.

Mission control was the usual combination of efficiency and buzz. The scientists and engineers were busy monitoring the data from the engines and the space station. The computer displays looked like 3D movies. As launch time got closer, the room got quieter.

Soon, Elon could hear his own heartbeat. The words of the countdown punctuated the hush.

Two, one, zero, ignition.

Falcon 9 Full Thrust blazed, then lifted calmly into the night. As it did, Elon pushed away memories of launches that hadn't gone right. The previous year, an unmanned test of the Dragon capsule had actually exploded. Months of further testing and asking questions stopped a repeat.

Elon watched, heart pumping, mind imagining what was happening inside the rocket and its Dragon capsule. The whoosh of liquid oxygen into ignition chambers. G-forces jamming the pilots in their seats. Stage One separated and began its descent back to Earth. Then Dragon left stage two behind, and began its approach to the Space Station.

Slowly, adjusted by computers and the two pilots, Dragon closed the distance to the International Space Station. Soon, Elon could see the hatch where Dragon would join onto the space station. It was on dozens of screens in mission control. The astronauts in the space station watched, too, as did those in Dragon. The hatch loomed closer and closer. Red crosses appeared, marking exactly where Dragon had to join. Matter-of-fact voices counted the meters down, nearer and nearer.

To Elon, it all appeared like many movies in his head. There were pictures of the two spaceships from outside as they made their spins match. There were pictures of the pulses of electricity that made Dragon's thrusters tweak the vessel's direction. There were pictures of the cooling liquid going from tanks into the astronaut's spacesuits.

A second countdown started. It came from the Dragon crew themselves as they steered the final seconds. Perfect to a hair's breadth, the hatch grew bigger on the screens till, with a kiss, it shimmered and went still.

A voice spoke from inside the space station. "Mission Control, we caught a Dragon by its tail."

Elon's eyes misted. He almost didn't hear the rising cheers. For a moment, there was rest.

He tweeted about the triumph: *First manned mission not by a private business. Our next rockets, Falcon Heavy and Starship, are ready to test now. Mars is on our way!*

He basked in the success of the rockets. They were like Genius Boy used to imagine in his room when he was reading his books and putting himself in the place of the hero.

He had accomplished so many of his dreams, but his eyes still faced forward to his biggest and most daring dream. To create a new world where humans could live:

Mars.

There was no doubt in his mind that he could do it.

He looked at the starry night and smiled.

*"I say something, and then it usually happens.
Maybe not on schedule, but it usually happens."*

~ *Elon Musk* ~

READ NEXT THE INTERNATIONAL BESTSELLER

Her parents didn't want her to do it. Her classmates refused to join her. Passersby expressed pity and bemusement at the sight of the pigtailed teenager who sat alone on the cobblestones in front of the Swedish Parliament with a hand-painted banner saying *School Strike for Climate*.

Before she went on strike, fifteen-year-old Greta Thunberg refused to speak and eat. She had no friends and no purpose in life. But one day she decided to act. A year later, her strike sparked a global movement with millions of followers who shared a common goal: Save the planet. Now.

Being Different is a Superpower is the heartfelt story of one family's love and devotion to each other and their quest for a better world.